Celtic Quilt Designs II
The Children of Lir

by Philomena Durcan.

Celtic Design Company, Sunnyvale, California.

Prined in China and Published by Celtic Design Company, Sunnyvale, CA.

Book Design by Colm Sweetman
Photography by Sharon Risendorph and Colm Sweetman
Illustrations by Colm Sweetman
Introduction by Philomena with Pat Flynn-Kyser
Copy editing by Crystal Chow
Printed by Regent Printing Co., Hong Kong

First Edition

Library of Congress Catalog Card No.: 2002095944
Library of Congress Cataloging-in-Publication Data
Durcan, Philomena
Celtic Quilt Designs II: The Children of Lir.

1. Applique - Patterns.   2. Quilts - Celtic
3. Patchwork - Patterns 4. Designs - Interlace
5. Quilting Techniques - Bias Bar Applique
6. Fabric Art

ISBN 0-9631982-3-8 (softcover)

Celtic Design Company,
P.O. Box 2643,
Sunnyvale, CA 94087.

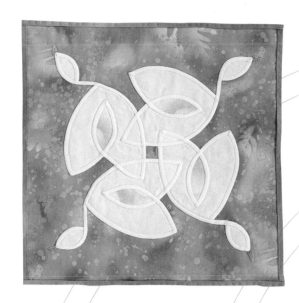

Welcome Welcome to another book exploring Celtic interlace designs. When *Celtic Quilt Designs* was published over 20 years ago, it was the start of a great journey of interweaving Celtic designs and friendships from around the world that has enriched my life tremendously. My sincere thanks to all of you.

My early years of teaching Celtic quilting can only be described as exciting, scary and wonderful. The whole range of emotions was at play. The designs were new and so was the concept itself, and this generated a lot of interest among quilters. Rather than considering myself solely as the teacher, however, I felt we were all learning together. It was and is so much fun.

I have learned a lot from my students. Each brought her or his own skills and techniques to the table. I find quilters love to share what works for them. Every class I have given has been a learning experience, but I picked up most of the tricks of the trade from my wonderful Studio 12 sewing group. We have been meeting together over the past 25 years, sharing quilting techniques and our lives. They are all outstanding quilters and seamstresses and wonderful supporting friends as well.

Two of my designs from my first book on Celtic quilt designs.

Below, one of the spiral patterns from *Celtic Spirals.*

In my two books and stencil kit that followed *Celtic Quilt Designs – Celtic Spirals, A Celtic Garden* and *Celtic Rose Window –* I was able to explore other forms of Celtic art. The spiral probably is only predated by the circle as an art form.

In working on *Celtic Spirals,* I was delighted that so many designs could be made from one master pattern, but 1 was faced with color challenges. As a result, I took many color and design classes at my local junior college and found the study very interesting. Our class projects were geared to help us become familiar with the color wheel and to work on a variety of color scales and harmonies. These and other classes have given me the freedom to experiment with any selection I chose from the color wheel.

My love affair with flowers allowed me to "paint" with fabric in *A Celtic Garden* and combine the floral motif with interlace design. I was following a tradition of floral motif in first-century Celtic art as expressed on the

magnificent gold torc, the Broighter collar. This collar embodies curved form, trumpet spirals and floral motifs. The Celts were known in the classical world by the elegantly elaborate torcs they wore.

Celtic Rose Window is a whole-cloth stencil kit (GD 1004) using five stencils that I designed for StenSource International Inc., and market through their company. The inspiration for this project came from discussions with Bonnie Benjamin, president of StenSource Inc., on the need for a whole-cloth Celtic quilt. The stained-glass windows in churches throughout Europe became the focus of my attention as I worked on the design. In addition to whole-cloth quilting, these stencil designs can be used with Celtic bias applique or trapunto in a variety of sizes.

Now, in *Celtic Quilt Designs II: The Children of Lir,* I have come full circle, returning to the traditional interlace and presenting 24 new Celtic interlace designs. In the course of making the quilt, more Celtic interlace designs emerged. Working once again with my nephew Colm Sweetman, a graphic designer, more designs evolved and soon we were off again on another publishing trip. Many of the designs are new ones of our own, others were inspired by the historic *Book of Kells,* the Ardagh chalice and the Tara brooch.

My further inspiration for this fourth book is the magical story of "The Children of Lir," an Irish legend that has enchanted young and old for centuries. I was moved to create a quilt with interlace design that matched the characters in the story.

I hope you, my readers and students, enjoy applying the designs as much as I enjoyed creating them. Further, I hope you encounter delight as you work with these reflections of my Celtic roots.

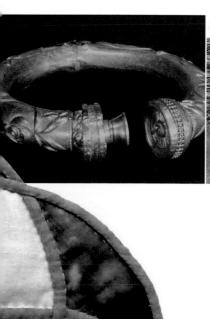

The Broighter collar with its floral pattern.
Patterns in walls in the west of Ireland.
Patterns in fields in the west of Ireland.
Above, anemones from *A Celtic Garden.*

Celtic Quilt Designs II: The Children of Lir continues my fascination with Celtic design. In preparing for this book, I researched many books on Irish myths and legends. I have always been enchanted by magical stories such as "The Taking of the Fairy Mounds," "The Wooing of Etain" and "The Fate of the Children of Lir," and many many more. I chose "the Children of Lir" because when I visited my niece Gráinne and her family in Portland, Oregon, her children were reading and discussing it. Happy memories of my own childhood stirred a desire in me to design a quilt depicting this legend.

In working on the designs in this book, once again I was drawn to the early Christian period and the art treasures it produced. Celtic art came alive again in the fifth century when Christianity entered Ireland. For the next 500 years Celtic and Christian art and symbols merged into truly unique art forms. Zig zags, diamonds, spirals, triangles, squares and interlace were used in stunning forms. Among them, interlace especially caught my imagination and inspired me.

I drew from the illuminated manuscripts that combined Celtic and Christian symbols in gold and silver and brilliant color. The books of Durrow, Kells and Lindisfane are magnificent examples of this early art and may be seen at Trinity College in Dublin and at the British Museum in London. They are illustrated with interlace patterns, facinating animal forms and brilliant hues. The *Book of Kells* has been described as "the work of angels not of man" (G. Frank Mitchell, *Treasures of Irish Art 1500 B.C. to 1500 A.D*). (Ref. 1)

The old cloak fastenings typical of the Celts were beautiful adornments. Though not Christian, the Tara Brooch is covered with detailed design. Like the Ardagh Chalice, its details and materials are of superior quality.

The Chalice is considered the finest example of eighth century metal work ever found in Ireland and was discovered by a young boy digging potatoes over 100 years ago in Ardagh, County Limerick. The Chalice is covered with filigree, engraving, cloisonne and enameling.

Featured here are photos of a few of the great works I have mentioned. In seeing them, you can readily see why the Celtic forms are so compelling and perhaps understand how they came to be my inspiration.

Celtic Sampler 2, 1999, 54" x 76", made by Philomena Durcan, quilted by Nancy Partridge.

The Ardagh chalice above. The spiral and diamond forms carved into the entrance stone at Newgrange. Left, a detail of the Chi-Rho page from the Book of Kells.

The Children of Lir

A thousand years before Christ, King Lir of Sid Finnachaid hoped to become High King of all Ireland. However, he was passed over by the chieftains in favor of King Bodb Deary and was so angered he left without pledging allegiance to the new High King. Many in the assembly wanted to pursue him and burn his home, but King Bodb restrained them, choosing to avoid the bloodshed that surely would have ensued if Lir was forced to defend his home turf.

Years later Lir was inconsolable when his beloved wife died. King Bodb chose to use this opportunity to make peace with his subject and so proposed that Lir take one of his own stepdaughters to be his wife.

Touched by the gesture, Lir chose Aobh and wed her at Loch Deary amid much celebration. They returned to his home at Sid Finnachaid, where they lived happily and ultimately produced twins, a girl they named Finola and a boy they named Aebh. Later they were blessed by another set of twins, sons they named Fiachra and Conn.

Tragically, the young mother died during this second birth, and her husband again was grief-stricken. Though heartbroken himself, when High King Bodb learned of Lir's second tragedy, he offered another stepdaughter, Aoife, to be wife to Lir and stepmother to her sister's children. This arrangement worked for a time and Aoife was a tender mother to her niece and nephews.

However, in time she became jealous of the attention drawn by the two sets of handsome young twins. She took them to swim in Lake Darva. Once they were in the water, she used a druid wand to transform the children into four white swans. She let them retain their human voices to sing the finest music heard in all of Ireland.

But the curse went further. They were to spend 300 years on the benevolent waters of Lake Darva, then 300 years on the stormy Sea of Moyle, which lay between Ireland and Scotland, and finally 300 years on the icy waters of Inis Glora.

The spell would not be broken until a prince of the north married a princess of the south, and a holy man named Patrick brought his teachings to Ireland and Christian bells rang.

King Bodb was so angry at the loss of his friend's children that he cast a spell on Aoife, making her a witch of the air for all time.

Mountains in the west and Inis Glora far off shrouded in cloud in the Sea of Moyle.

The first 300 years passed peacefully with the descendants of Lir and Bodb coming often to Lake Darva to hear the sweet singing of the four swans. The next 300 years were miserable on the Sea of Moyle, where they were isolated and their feathers often froze. The final period on the Inis Glora was terrible indeed, for the water froze solid and the birds were buffeted mercilessly by torrential winds. Finola comforted her brothers by urging them to put their trust in God who would bring comfort to them.

Eventually the 900 years passed and the swans were free to fly home to Sid Finnachaid. To their horror, their father's palace was in ruins. They spent years flying forlornly over Ireland until finally Saint Patrick came to spread the word of Christianity.

One of his followers, Saint Kennock, founded an oratory near Inis Glora. On a particular morning as the matins bells rang, the swans heard them and joined them in singing. Saint Kennock heard the heavenly music as he prayed, and God revealed to him that its source was the lost children of Lir. He had heard their sad story and invited the swans to pray with him the next day. When the oratory bells rang again, their feathers dropped and the swans were changed back into human form.

However, they were old and shriveled and wizened and soon after their baptism by Saint Kennock, they died. Honoring Fiola's last request, he buried the four of them together in a grave outside his chapel on Inis Glora. A stone pillar with their names in ogham letters was erected on their grave. Immediately Saint Kennock had a vision of four radiantly innocent and joyous children smiling at him and then taking flight a final time, upward to heaven.

(a)

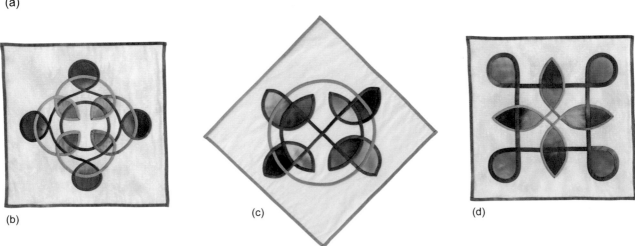

(b)

(c)

(d)

(a) The Children of Lir 2001, 42" x 42",
made by Philomena Durcan.
(b) Bofin, (c) Toirc (d) Tobber.
(e) Celtic Sampler 3, 2002, 62" x 78",
made by Philomena Durcan.

(e)

The bulk of this book is made up of Celtic interlace designs. There are 24 different designs in all, with complete cutting and illustrated applique instructions. Many of these designs were directly inspired by the story of Lir's children. The crown in my design symbolizes King Lir, the serpent represents Aoife the wicked stepmother, the swans are the children, the bells are the breaking of the spell, and the cross symbolizes the birth of Christianity in Ireland.

Note that each cut-out piece is shaded and directional arrows have been added to assist in laying down the bias trim.

Each design is sized for a 14" x 14" finished block; however, this can be scaled up or down using a pantograph tracing tool, available from most art stores.

The tools you will need are described later. Follow the step-by-step illustrated instructions for assembling the block and appliqueing the bias trim using the Celtic Design Company bias-bar technique. It is quite effective for adding a three-dimensional effect to your work, yet it is easy enough for beginners to use.

The sections on Color and Design and Fabric discuss the process of choosing fabric and colors to create special effects. Careful selection of color and fabric will make the difference between a finished piece that appears to be flat and inanimate, and one that is vibrant and alive.

The section on Finishing Techniques gives you ideas for assembling and quilting your finished piece, such as how to arrange and separate the blocks or selecting which kind of borders are pleasing to you.

Because this is a design book, there are no instructions on how to assemble the quilt. However, I have listed several excellent books that cover these instructions in detail.

Illustrations of various types of finished pieces are included throughout the book to give you inspiration and approaches for your own work and to show the splendor of Celtic art that is such an integral part of my Irish heritage.

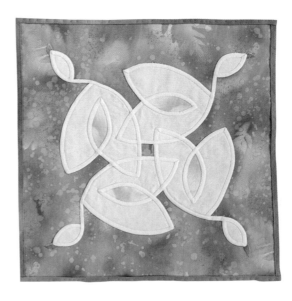

There are 10 basic steps you need to perform to complete your applique project. They are presented in the order in which the task will be performed, and will give you a comprehensive overview.

Step 1. Collect all the tools and supplies listed on the next two pages.

Step 2. Copy the chosen design pattern from the book onto 11" x 17" tracing vellum. If you are using several of the interlace designs, repeat the process for each of them.

Step 3. Trace the chosen design onto the background fabric.

Step 4. Make paper templates for cutting out the applique pieces.

Step 5. Cut out the applique pieces and baste them to the traced design on your background block.

Step 6. Make the bias.

Step 7. Applique the bias to the design.

Step 8. Assemble the appliqued blocks.

Step 9. Trace your background quilting design onto the front of the quilt. (Celtic Design Company stencils can be used to help with this.)

Step 10. Add the batting and backing, then quilt the final work in the usual manner.

Tools Bias applique is fine work, and it requires fine tools. It is important to have the right tools and supplies to do the job. Here is a list of items you will need to get started.

Thread to match your fabric, or 100% silk applique thread. YLI size #100.

Needles, Piecemakers Applique #12. Quilting needles, John James #10 or #12. Sharps are both excellent and highly recommended.

A thimble to protect your fingers.

Three pairs of scissors, one to cut paper, one to cut fabric and one for close trimming.

A rotary cutter and cutting board for cutting bias.

A see-through Omnigrid 6" x 24" ruler that measures down to 1/8".

A foam-core pinboard 18"x 24" (available in any art supply store).

An iron and ironing board.

A tracing pad, vellum (preferred).

A washable Ultimate Marking pencil for quilters, or a #3 hard lead pencil.

A fine black marking pen.

A 1/4" Celtic Design Company metal bias bar for making bias to outline the design patterns; 1/8", 3/16", 3/8", 1/2", 5/8" and 3/4" metal bias bars for embellishing or special effects, depending upon your design.

Today's choices of fabric are fabulous and seemingly endless. A visit to your local quilt stores will acquaint you with a large selection. Most shops usually carry all the major fabric manufacturers.

I have also used wonderful fabrics from several smaller specialty suppliers, such as Alaska Dye Works, Artspoken Yardage, *Fabricstodyefor.com* and Skydyes. Mottled fabrics in light and dark tones of the same color are wonderful to work with, as are monotone or variegated tie-dyed fabrics. The mottled and tie-dyed fabrics are excellent for adding movement and depth. If you are new to fabric art, you might consider buying several "fat quarters" (18" x 22") of fabric of various colors and patterns from different manufacturers and experiment with them. Most quilt stores have a large selection of "fat quarters" available.

In the interlace designs in this book I used a solid color for the bias trim or two solid colors that blended, and I combined different widths of bias. This added interest and dimension.

I recommend 100% cotton fabric for both quiltmaking and for the bias applique.

Here several similar designs are shown. Each use different combinations of fabric and color.

Color and design

The approach I have taken in this book involves using the color wheel. I choose the colors I like and work from there. Split complements, which are those having opposite relationships, have a refreshing look. Analogous colors that are closely related to each other on the color wheel are pleasing to the eye. Complementary shades that are opposite each other on the color wheel provide vibrancy.

Try using different values, such as several hues of purple, rather than contrasting complementary colors, such as red and green. Experiment with triads, which I have found to have a unique beauty. In this case, combine every third color on the wheel and work with shades and tones of them. Too, it is important that each of your blocks contains a light, a medium and a dark value of the fabrics you choose. Each of my quilts and color samples employ this approach.

Since color, like life, is a process, I highly recommend that you take lots of classes on color. There are also excellent books on the subject that I have referenced.

It is a good idea to make several "mock" samples of your finished piece until you find the color scheme that pleases you most. Usually the finished blocks dictate the sashing and border colors to use. Be sure to figure in those sashings and borders in estimating the overall size of your piece.

analogous

complementary

split complement

complementary

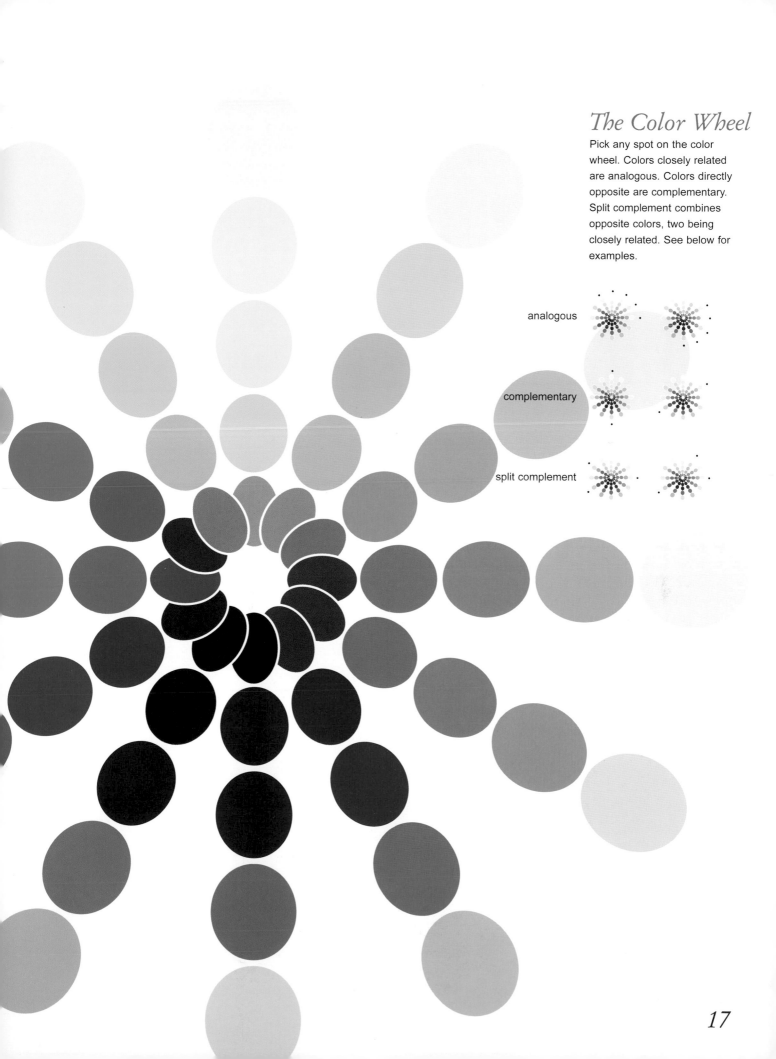

The Color Wheel

Pick any spot on the color wheel. Colors closely related are analogous. Colors directly opposite are complementary. Split complement combines opposite colors, two being closely related. See below for examples.

analogous

complementary

split complement

Tracing from the book

attach vellum to a design | mark the center and begin tracing | mark the dotted line

Tracing to the fabric

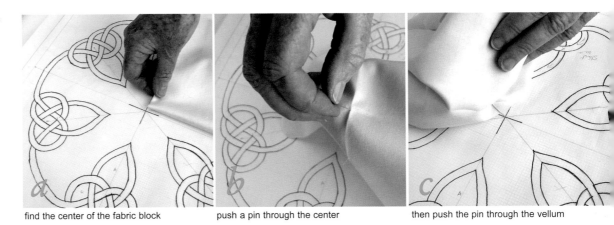

find the center of the fabric block | push a pin through the center | then push the pin through the vellum

Cut-outs

Estimated yardage

Size	Fabric
14"x 14" quilt block	1/2 to 2/3 yard of fabric
42"x 42" Lir quilt	7 yards of fabric
55"x 80" sampler	8 yards of fabric
64"x 80" sampler	8 1/2 yards of fabric

18

en match and trace the facing page   mark all corners too   repeat to complete the full design   now your design is complete

uare and secure   begin tracing to the fabric

Tracing from the book

Select a design. *1* First attach 16" x 16" vellum paper to the left-hand page and secure with paper clips. *2* Mark the center cross and corner and begin tracing the first quarter. *3* Add the dotted line. You now have completed one quarter of the design. *4* Remove the tracing and attach it to the right- hand facing page, matching the center and dotted line. *5* Continue to trace the next quarter. You will now have half a design completed. *6* Rotate your vellum paper and repeat the steps adding the third and fourth quarters. *7* You now have a completed design.

Tracing to the fabric

Place a sheet of foamcore board underneath your vellum tracing. This is an essential work surface. *a* Locate the center of a 15-inch square of fabric by folding it in half, then half again. Pinch the corner then open it out. The cross crease is the center. Match it with the center of your tracing. *b* Do this by pushing a pin through the center cross in the fabric *c* then into the foamcore board through the center cross of your traced vellum. *d* Flatten out the square of fabric and secure to the vellum with pins. *e* Begin lightly tracing the design to the fabric with a 3H pencil. If the fabric is dark, use a light box or attach the two to a window with the light coming through from behind. **Note:** Be careful to place the design on the vertical straight of the background fabric.

Cut-outs

Cut-outs are indicated in gray shading on patterns. *f* Trace the cut-outs to vellum using the **outside line** of the pattern as your guide. **Do not** trace to the inside line as your pieces will be too small to tuck under the bias trim. Now pin the traced vellum to your selected fabric and carefully cut out the applique pieces. *g* Pin the pieces, one by one, onto the design traced on to your background block. Baste to secure and remove pins.

19

Making 1/4" bias strips

fold your square

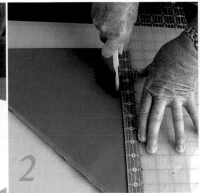

measure off 7/8" strips

cut strips

steam press

1 Measure off a square of fabric. Fold it in half diagonally to form a triangle. Press the fabric lightly along the fold with a hot iron. **Note:** It is very important that strips be cut along the diagonal fold of a true square of fabric. Fabric cut in any other way will not have the stretching properties to follow your pattern. *2* Using a seethrough ruler, measure 7/8" away from the fold. *3* Cut with a rotary cutter along the edge of the ruler to make a bias strip. Measure down another 7/8" and cut the next bias

Adding bias trim

start at an under section

miter bias at corners

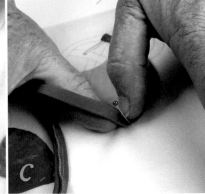

fold bias to face in new direction

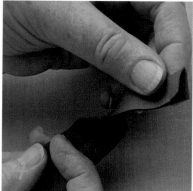

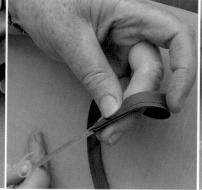

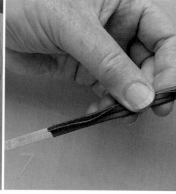

fold strip, right side facing out | machine sew | insert 1/4" bias bar | roll seam to center

strip, and so forth until all the fabric has been cut into strips. **Note:** Your first cut strip is on the fold. Cut through giving two strips. *4* Fold each strip of bias with right side facing out. *5* Machine sew 1/4"+ from the folded edge. You now have a tube strip of fabric. **Note:** There is no need to sew the strips of bias together to make one long piece of bias because the ends of the bias tuck under. *6* Now insert the 1/4" bias bar into each tube. *7* Roll the seam to the center of the flat side of the metal bar. *8* With the bias bar still inserted, steam press the tube with the seam down the center and with both seam edges facing to one side. Push the bar forward through the tube until the entire strip is pressed. You should now have a strip of bias 1/4" wide with the seam down the center of the backside ready to applique to your basted pattern.

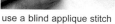

finger press the corner | use a blind applique stitch | make sure raw seam is facing out | do not sew down areas of overlap

a Start laying down your bias at an under section indicated by an arrow on the pattern. Do not pin down. Follow that direction. Lay the bias along the contour of the design. Sew down the **inside curve first** using a blind applique stitch. **Do not sew down the outside edge yet.** *b* At the places where the bias changes direction abruptly, miter the point at which the direction changes by placing a pin through the bias at that point and *c* folding the bias over to face in the new direction. *d* Finger press the bias in place. *e* Stitch it down using a blind applique stitch. *f* As you applique make sure that the raw seam on the bias is flaring outward on an outward curve. Important, sew down the inside curve first. *g* Do not sew down on areas of overlap at this time. Leave space for bias trim to run under. *h* Sew down the outside edge and overlap areas to complete the pattern.

(a)

(b)

(c)

22

(d)

(a) Layout for The Children of Lir quilt.

(b) Layout for a six block Celtic Sampler.

(c) Layout for The Children of Lir wall hanging.

(d) Layout for Celtic Sampler 3. (see page 11)

Pages 24 and 25

(e) Layout for Celtic Sampler 2. (see page 7)

(f) Layout for a twenty block Celtic Sampler.

24

Students' Gallery

(a)

(b)

26

(a) Bias Applique Rose Window 1998, 42" x 60", designed and made by Philomena Durcan, quilted by Mary Bertken. This was exhibited in Germany at the Quilts in Bloom art exhibit, 1999.

(b) Celtic Christmas wall hanging 2001, 12" x 40", from a stencil (CD 1113) made by Joan Blomquist. She hangs the wall hanging over her fireplace at Christmas time. Joan is new to quilting and is doing a beautiful job.

(c) Whole Cloth Celtic 1995, 60" x 60", quilted for me by April Murphy, who does beautiful work, trapunto and design by Philomena Durcan.

(d) Large Celtic Rose Window 1999, 80" x 80", made by Barbara Amedo for her daughter Susan, who loves things Irish. It won a blue ribbon at the Santa Clara Valley Quilt Fair 2000.

(c)

(d)

(e) Celtic Christmas Spiral sampler 2000, 54" x 54", made by Sherry Klootwyk from my book *Celtic Spirals* at a class I gave at the Sunnyvale Senior Center in California.

(f) A Celtic Floral Sampler 1997, 46"x 46", made by Pat Daughters from my book *A Celtic Garden,* at a class I gave at the Sunnyvale Senior Center.

(g) Roisin 2000, 21" x 21", made by Joan Blomquist from my book *Celtic Spirals.* She is now working on a quilt using the spiral designs.

(h) Poppy Block 2001, 20" x 20", (CD 754) made by Philomena Durcan as a class sample, design taken from my book *A Celtic Garden.*

(e)

(f)

28

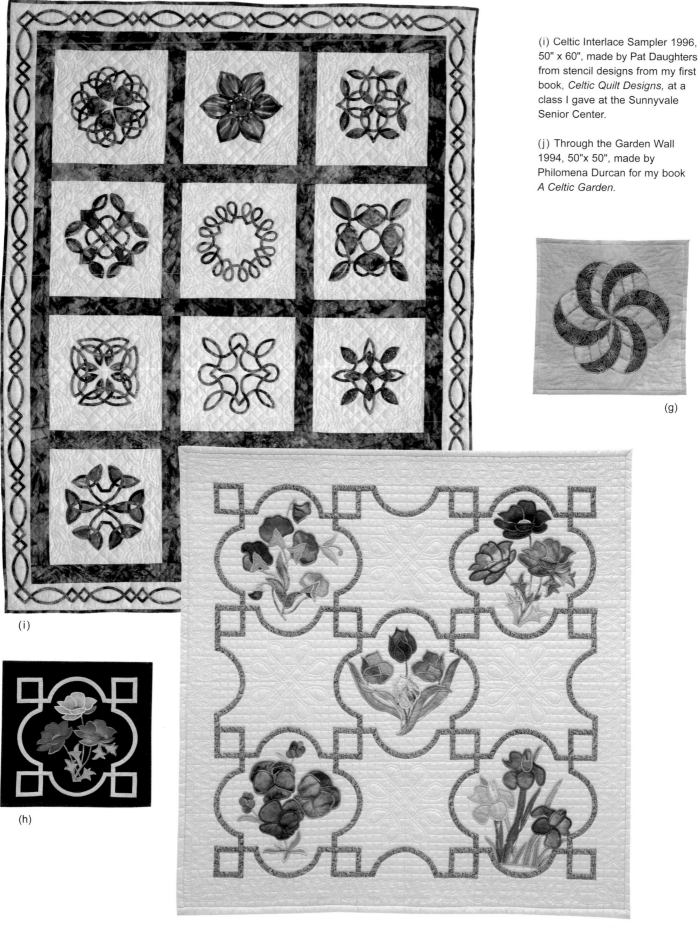

(i) Celtic Interlace Sampler 1996, 50" x 60", made by Pat Daughters from stencil designs from my first book, *Celtic Quilt Designs,* at a class I gave at the Sunnyvale Senior Center.

(j) Through the Garden Wall 1994, 50"x 50", made by Philomena Durcan for my book *A Celtic Garden.*

(g)

(i)

(h)

(j)

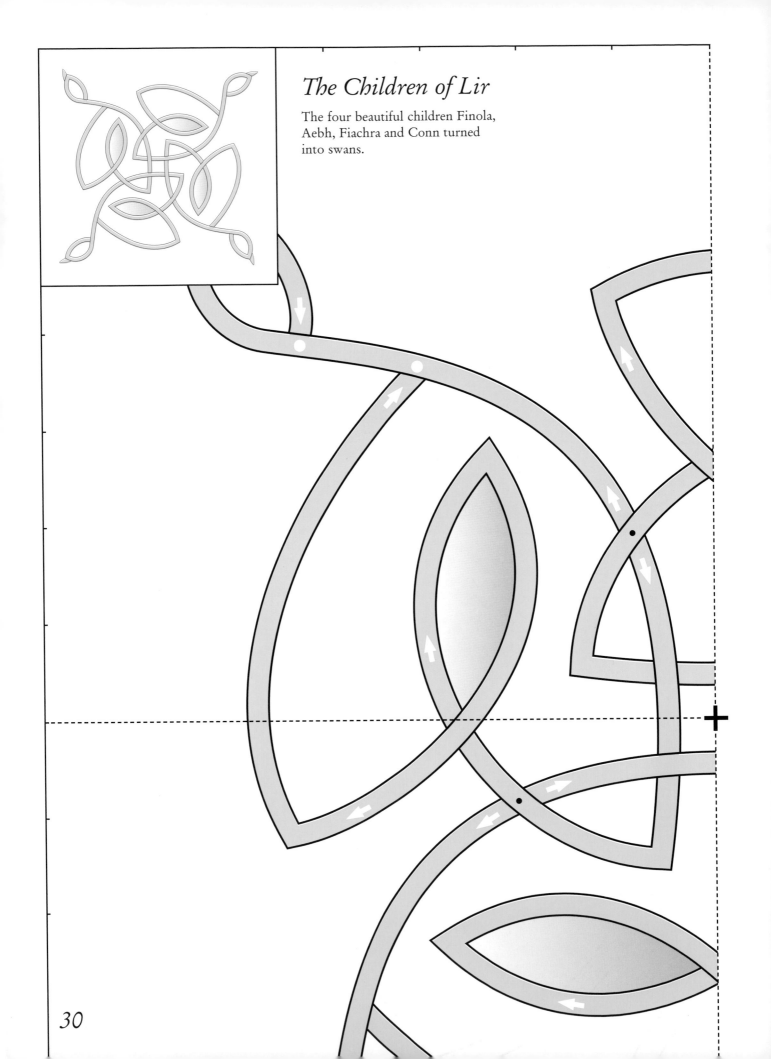

The Children of Lir

The four beautiful children Finola,
Aebh, Fiachra and Conn turned
into swans.

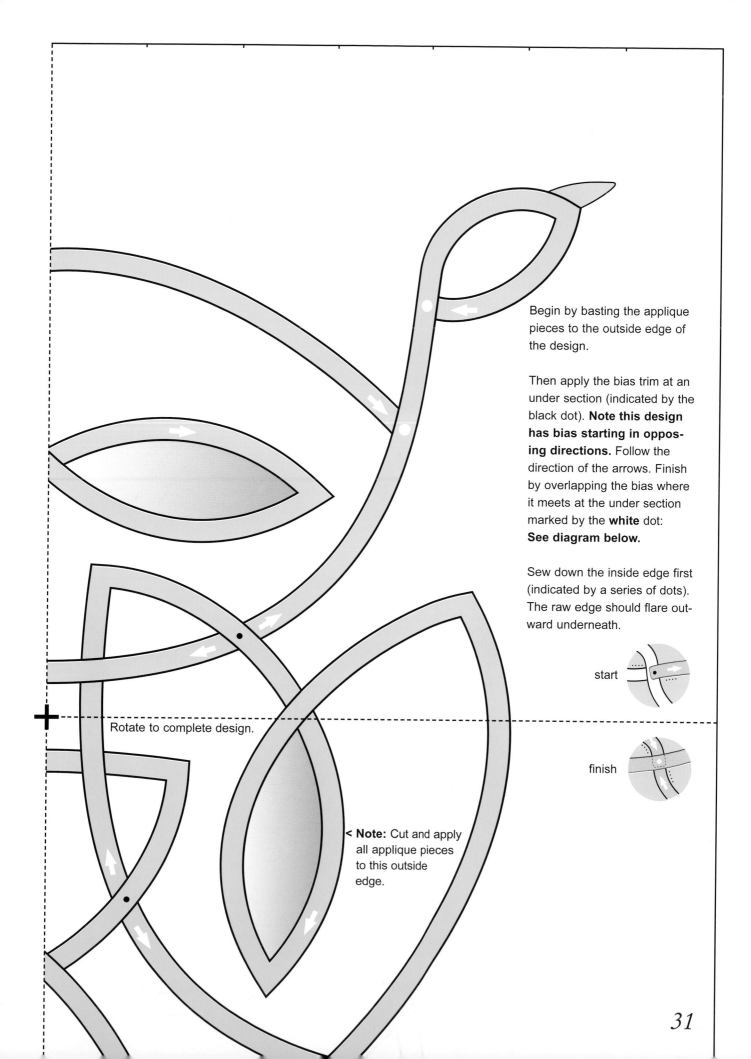

Begin by basting the applique pieces to the outside edge of the design.

Then apply the bias trim at an under section (indicated by the black dot). **Note this design has bias starting in opposing directions.** Follow the direction of the arrows. Finish by overlapping the bias where it meets at the under section marked by the **white** dot: **See diagram below.**

Sew down the inside edge first (indicated by a series of dots). The raw edge should flare outward underneath.

start

finish

Rotate to complete design.

< **Note:** Cut and apply all applique pieces to this outside edge.

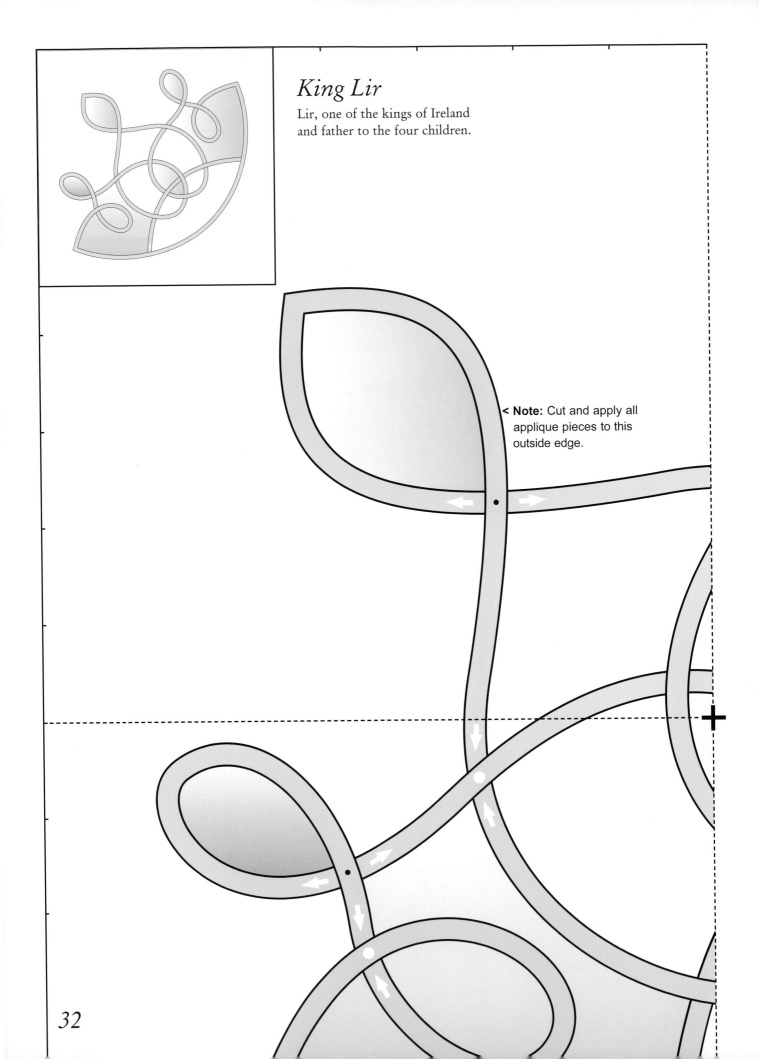

King Lir

Lir, one of the kings of Ireland and father to the four children.

< **Note:** Cut and apply all applique pieces to this outside edge.

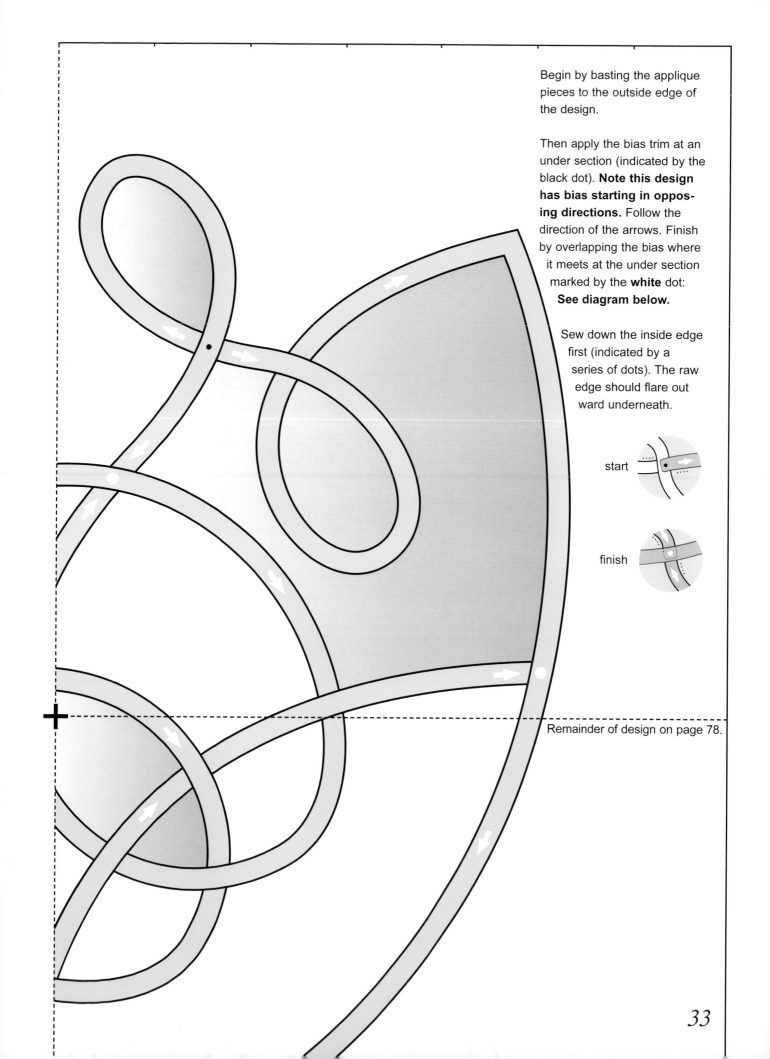

Begin by basting the applique pieces to the outside edge of the design.

Then apply the bias trim at an under section (indicated by the black dot). **Note this design has bias starting in opposing directions.** Follow the direction of the arrows. Finish by overlapping the bias where it meets at the under section marked by the **white** dot: **See diagram below.**

Sew down the inside edge first (indicated by a series of dots). The raw edge should flare out ward underneath.

start

finish

Remainder of design on page 78.

33

Aoife

The jealous stepmother who had
the children turned into swans at
Lake Darva.

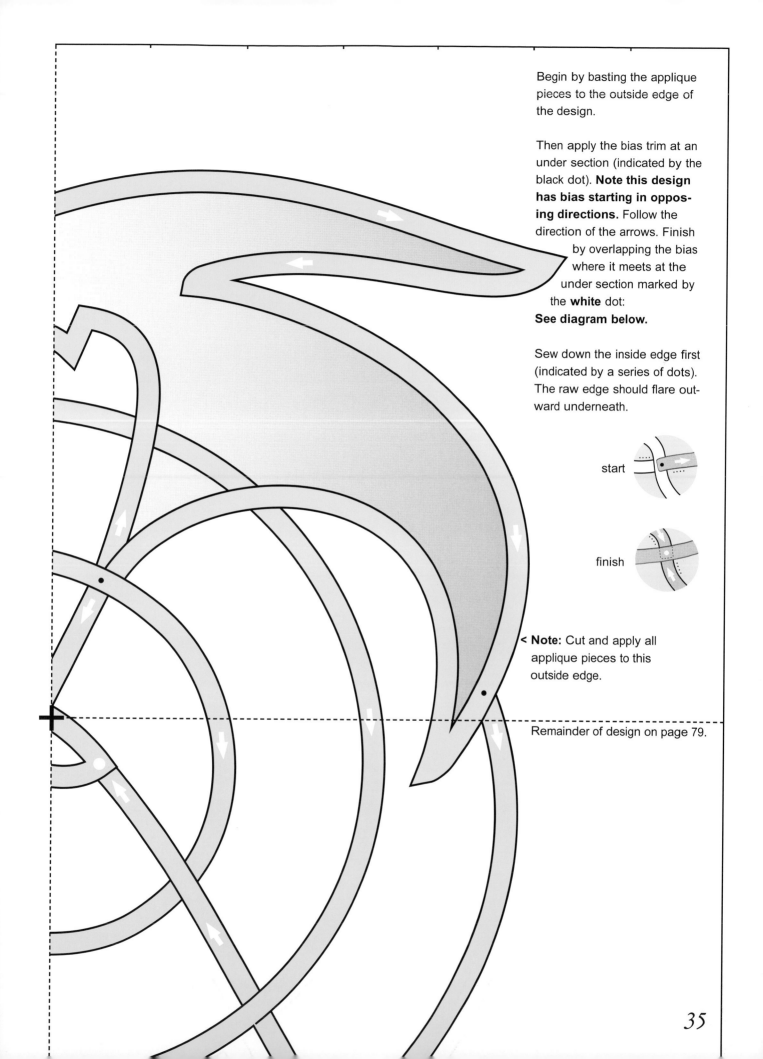

Begin by basting the applique pieces to the outside edge of the design.

Then apply the bias trim at an under section (indicated by the black dot). **Note this design has bias starting in opposing directions.** Follow the direction of the arrows. Finish by overlapping the bias where it meets at the under section marked by the **white** dot:
See diagram below.

Sew down the inside edge first (indicated by a series of dots). The raw edge should flare outward underneath.

start

finish

< **Note:** Cut and apply all applique pieces to this outside edge.

Remainder of design on page 79.

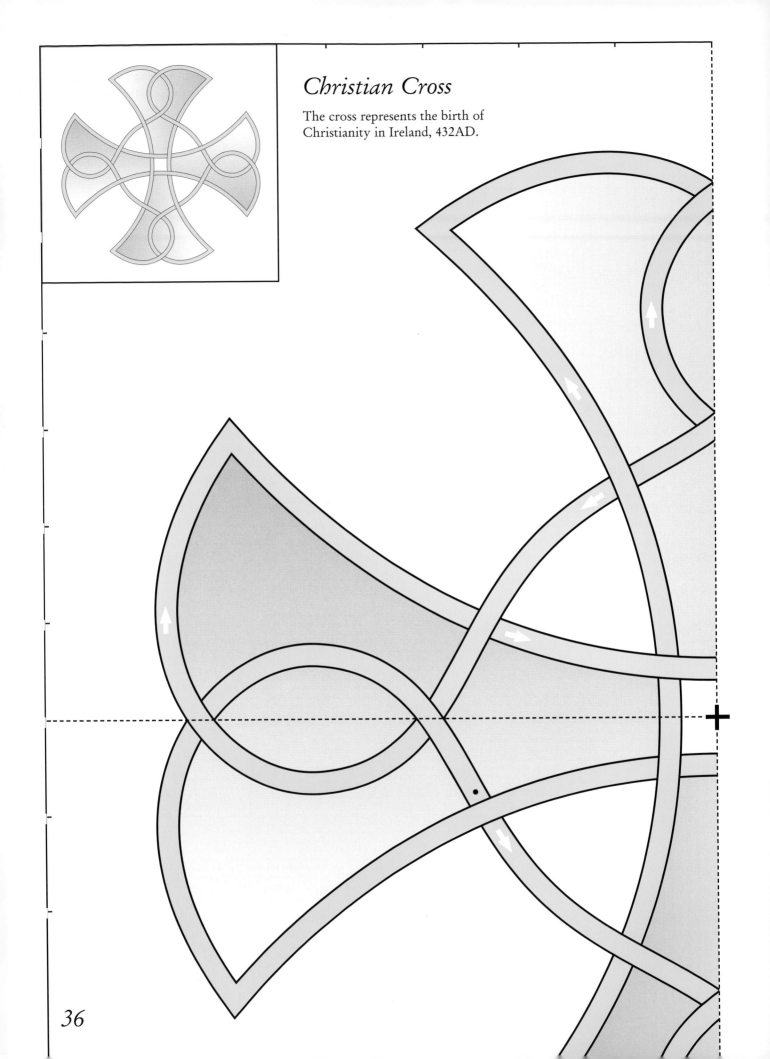

Christian Cross

The cross represents the birth of
Christianity in Ireland, 432AD.

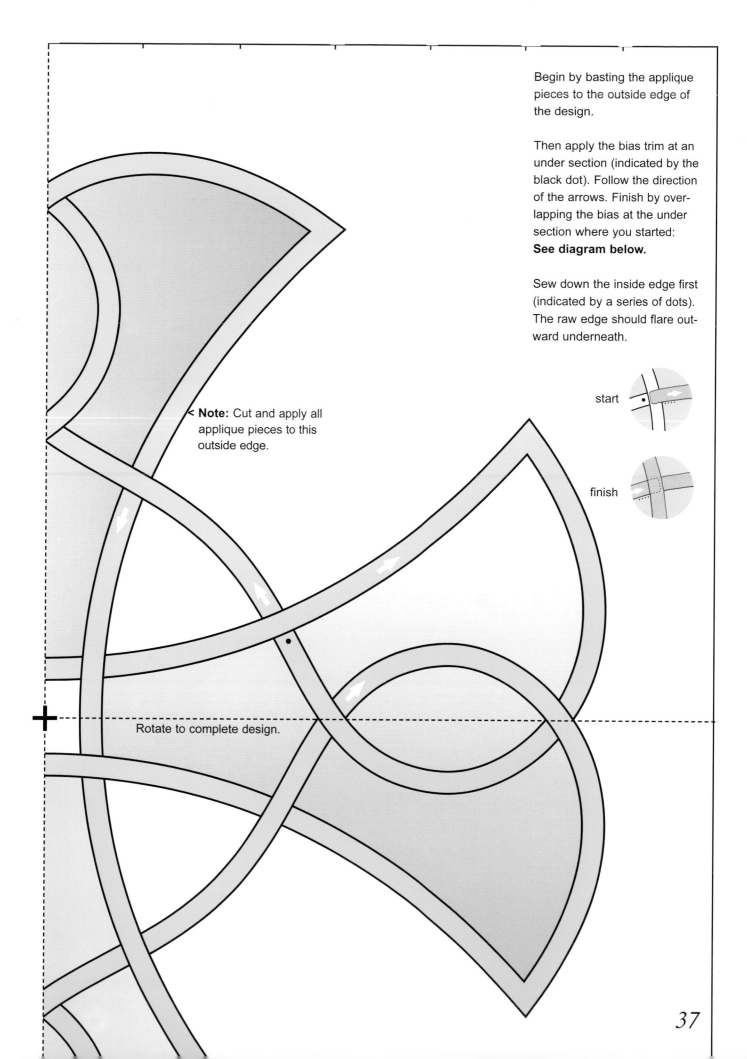

Begin by basting the applique pieces to the outside edge of the design.

Then apply the bias trim at an under section (indicated by the black dot). Follow the direction of the arrows. Finish by overlapping the bias at the under section where you started: **See diagram below.**

Sew down the inside edge first (indicated by a series of dots). The raw edge should flare outward underneath.

start

finish

◄ **Note:** Cut and apply all applique pieces to this outside edge.

Rotate to complete design.

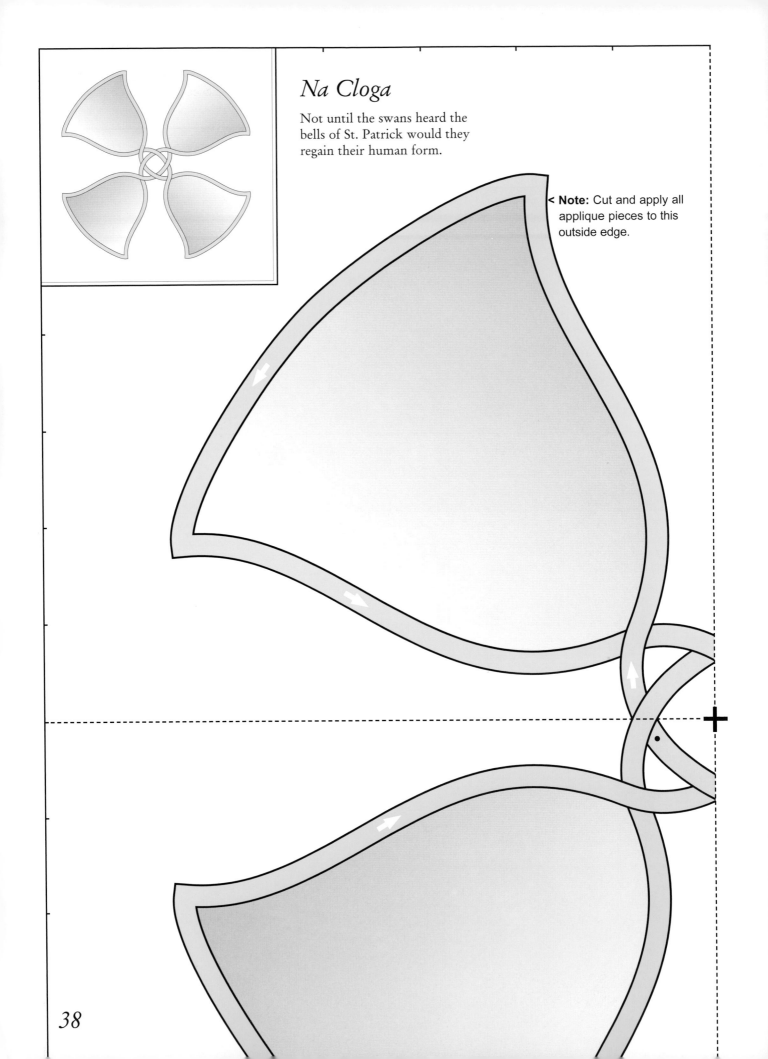

Na Cloga

Not until the swans heard the
bells of St. Patrick would they
regain their human form.

< **Note:** Cut and apply all
applique pieces to this
outside edge.

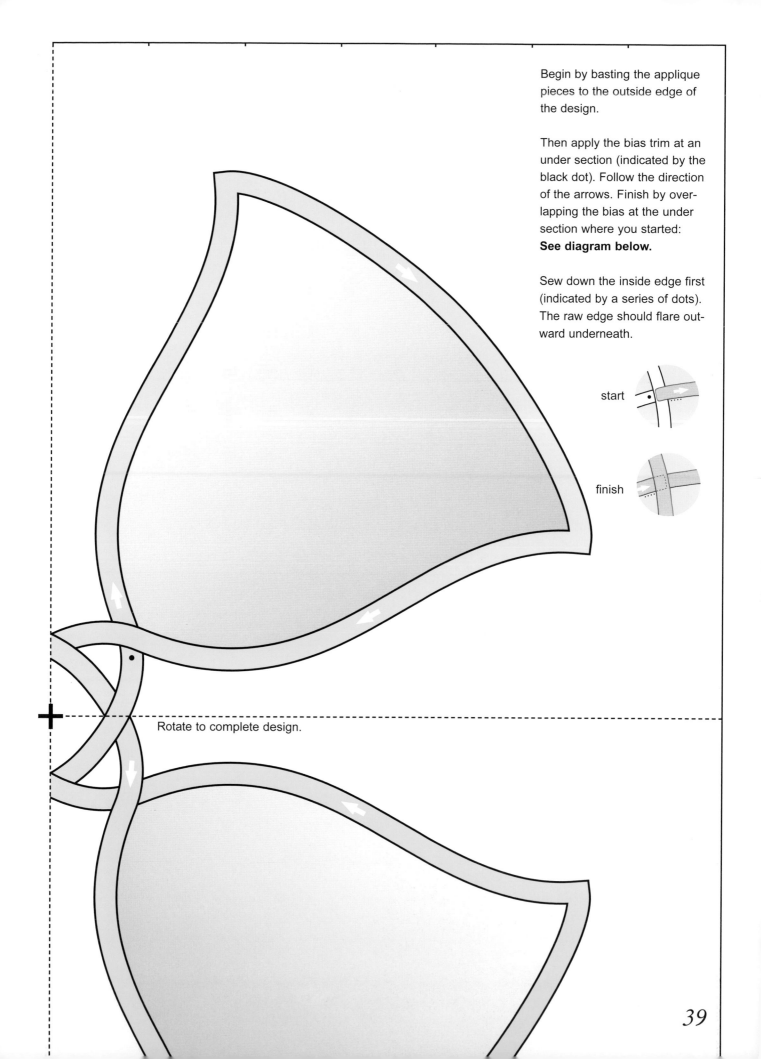

Begin by basting the applique pieces to the outside edge of the design.

Then apply the bias trim at an under section (indicated by the black dot). Follow the direction of the arrows. Finish by overlapping the bias at the under section where you started: **See diagram below.**

Sew down the inside edge first (indicated by a series of dots). The raw edge should flare outward underneath.

start

finish

Rotate to complete design.

39

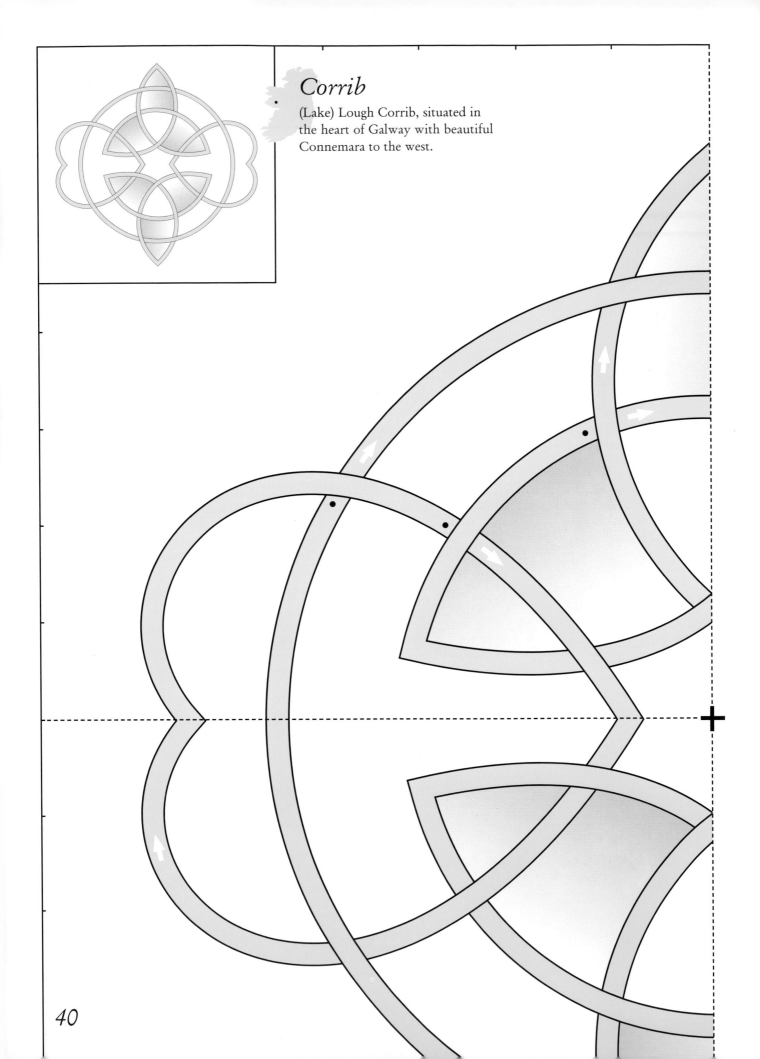

Corrib

(Lake) Lough Corrib, situated in the heart of Galway with beautiful Connemara to the west.

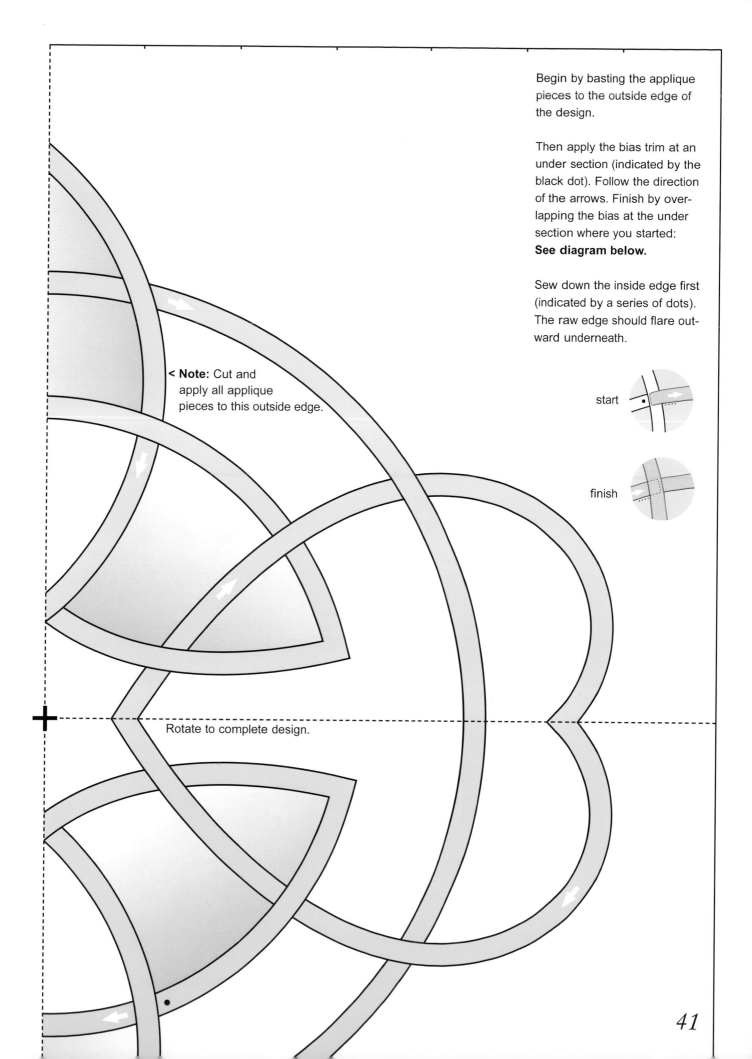

Begin by basting the applique pieces to the outside edge of the design.

Then apply the bias trim at an under section (indicated by the black dot). Follow the direction of the arrows. Finish by overlapping the bias at the under section where you started: **See diagram below.**

Sew down the inside edge first (indicated by a series of dots). The raw edge should flare outward underneath.

start

finish

< **Note:** Cut and apply all applique pieces to this outside edge.

Rotate to complete design.

41

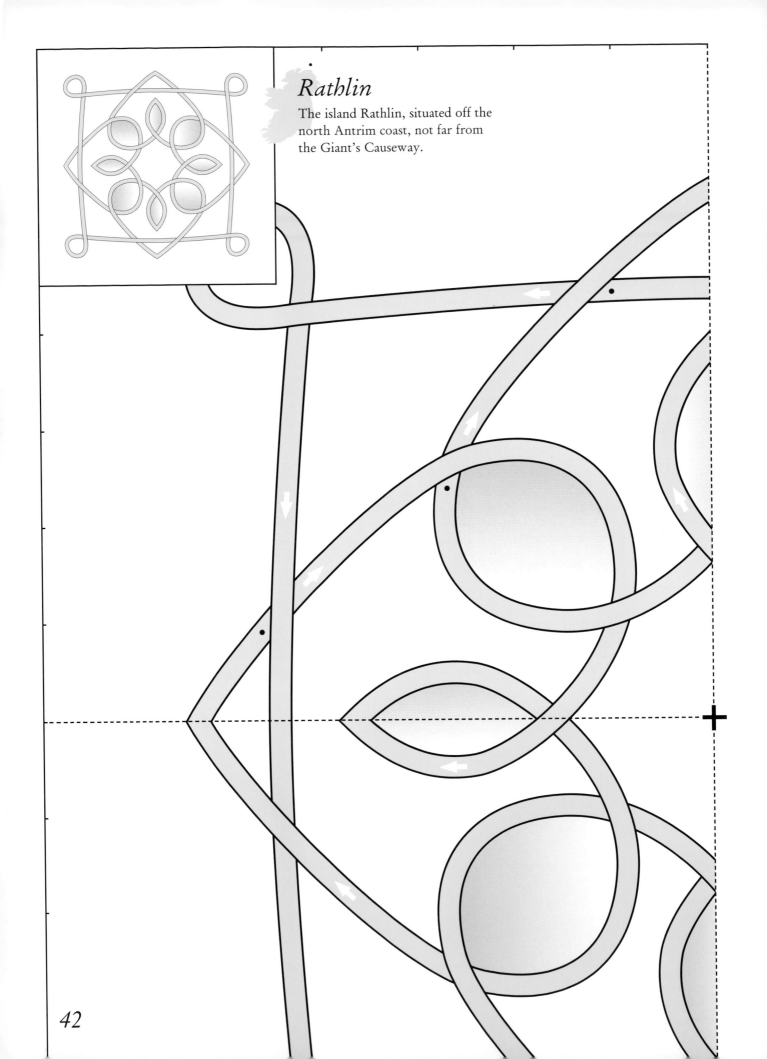

Rathlin

The island Rathlin, situated off the
north Antrim coast, not far from
the Giant's Causeway.

42

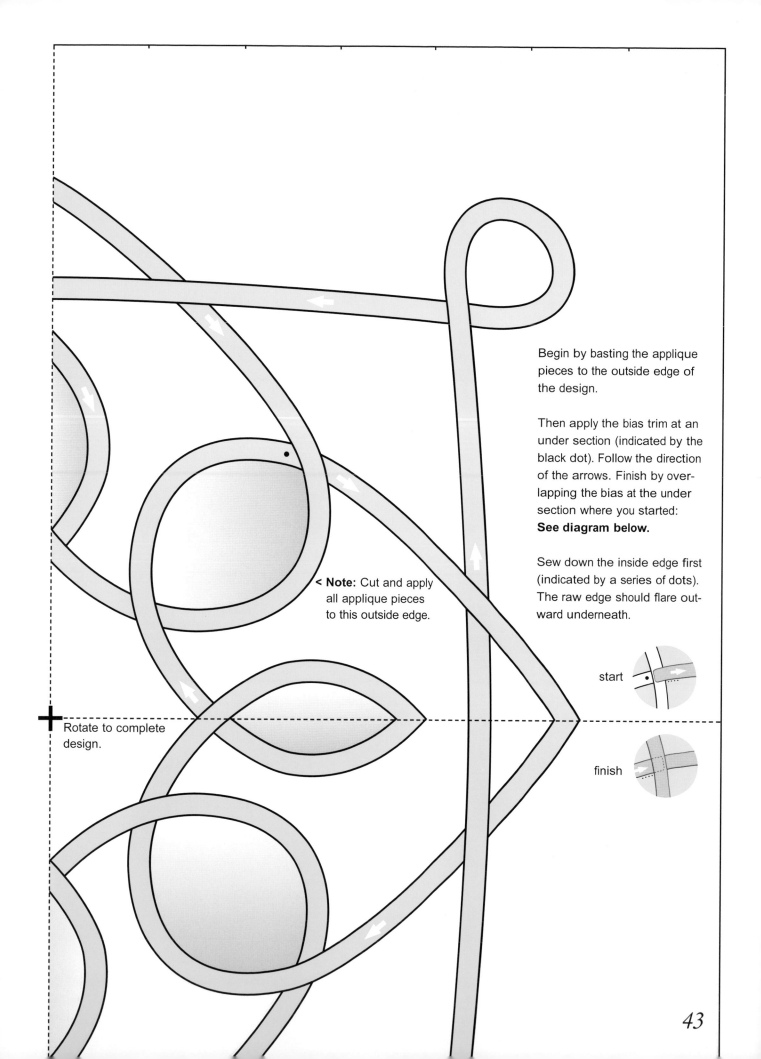

< **Note:** Cut and apply
all applique pieces
to this outside edge.

Rotate to complete
design.

Begin by basting the applique
pieces to the outside edge of
the design.

Then apply the bias trim at an
under section (indicated by the
black dot). Follow the direction
of the arrows. Finish by overlapping the bias at the under
section where you started:
See diagram below.

Sew down the inside edge first
(indicated by a series of dots).
The raw edge should flare outward underneath.

start

finish

Oirr

Innis Oirr, the smallest of the
Arran islands, looking back at the
cliffs of Moher in County Clare.

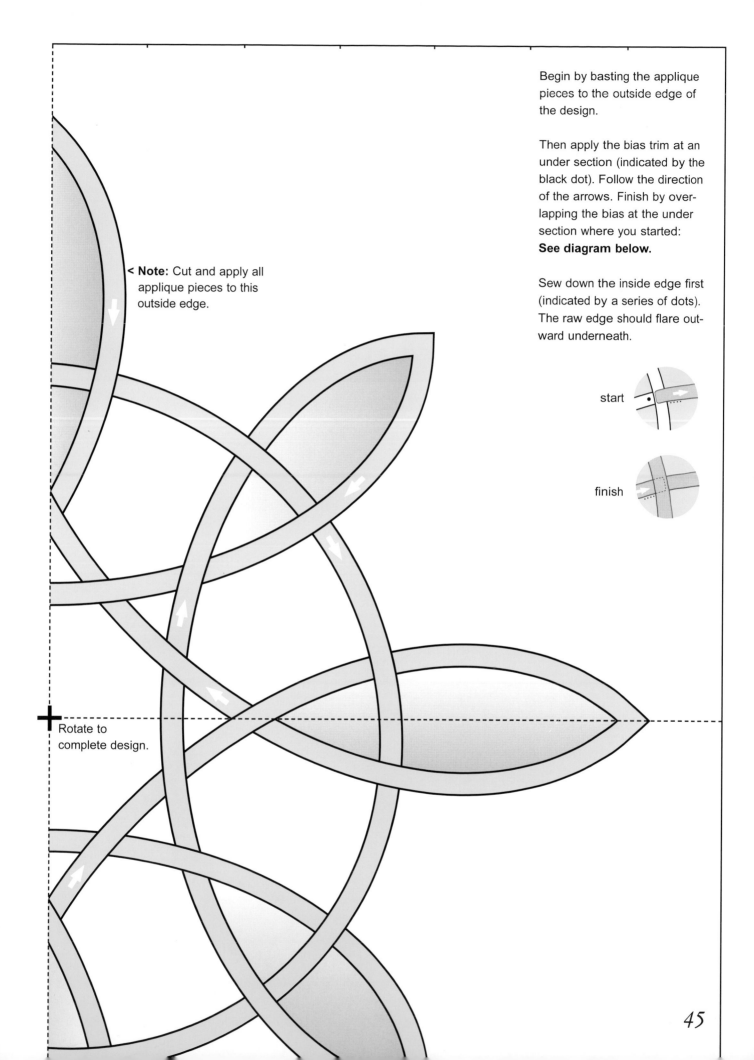

Begin by basting the applique pieces to the outside edge of the design.

Then apply the bias trim at an under section (indicated by the black dot). Follow the direction of the arrows. Finish by over-lapping the bias at the under section where you started: **See diagram below.**

Sew down the inside edge first (indicated by a series of dots). The raw edge should flare out-ward underneath.

start

finish

< **Note:** Cut and apply all applique pieces to this outside edge.

Rotate to complete design.

45

· *Gill*

(Lake) Lough Gill, situated in
Sligo with Benbulbin to the
north.

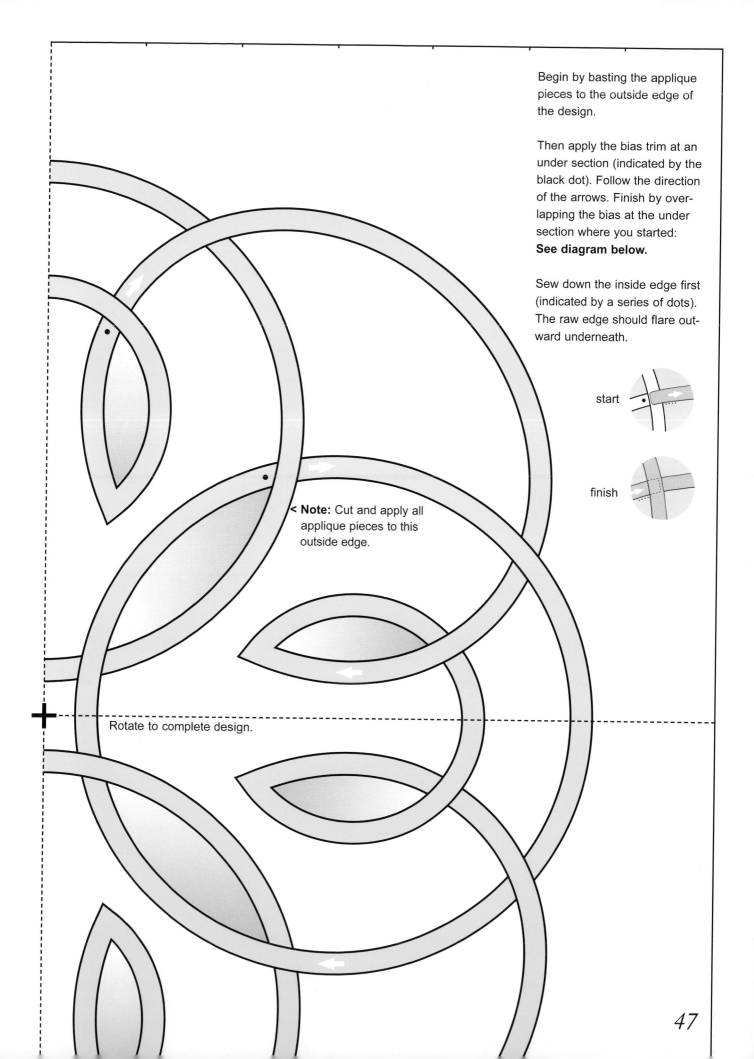

Begin by basting the applique pieces to the outside edge of the design.

Then apply the bias trim at an under section (indicated by the black dot). Follow the direction of the arrows. Finish by overlapping the bias at the under section where you started: **See diagram below.**

Sew down the inside edge first (indicated by a series of dots). The raw edge should flare outward underneath.

start

finish

< **Note:** Cut and apply all applique pieces to this outside edge.

Rotate to complete design.

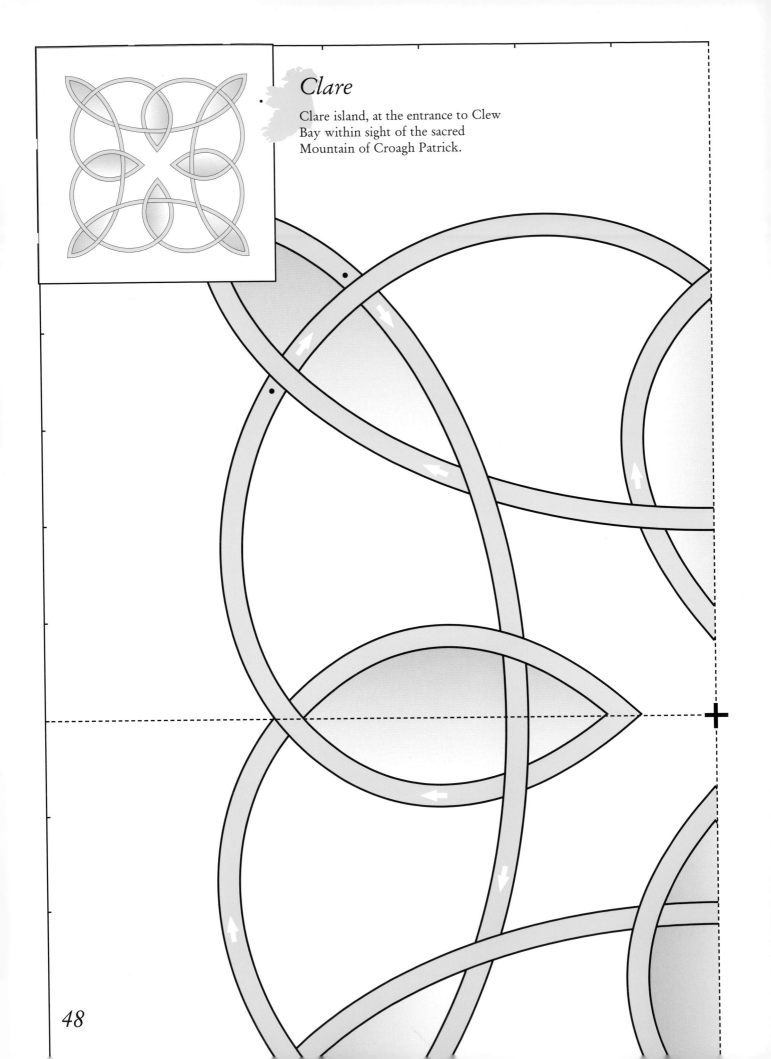

Clare

Clare island, at the entrance to Clew Bay within sight of the sacred Mountain of Croagh Patrick.

48

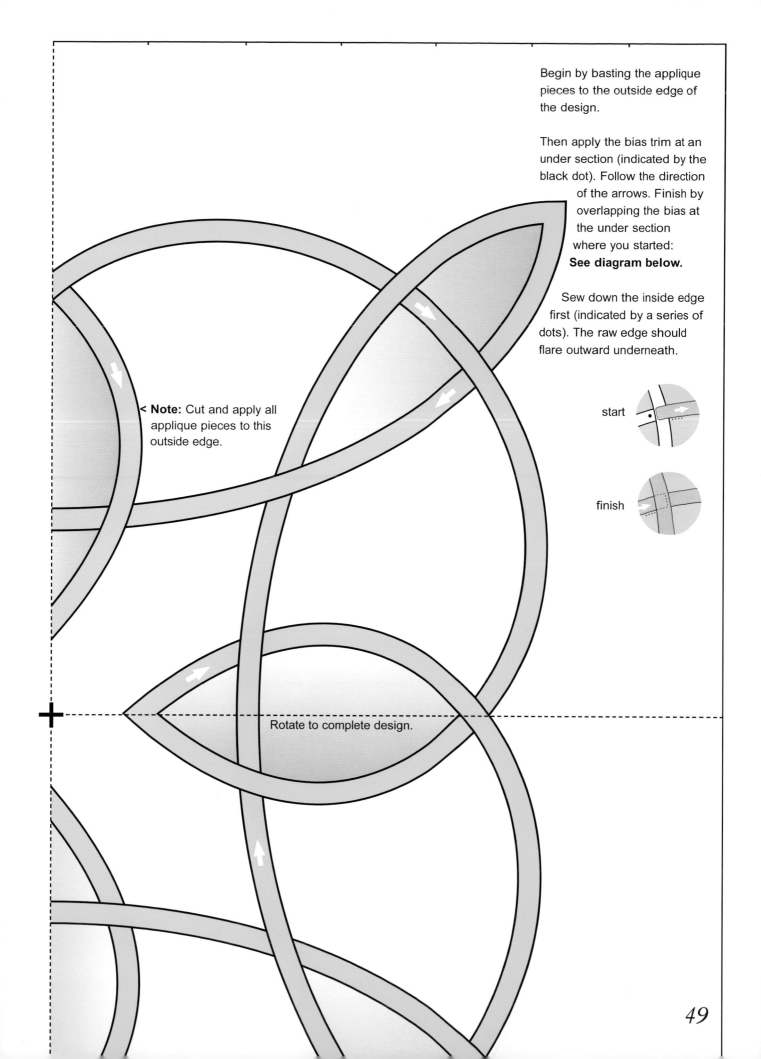

Begin by basting the applique pieces to the outside edge of the design.

Then apply the bias trim at an under section (indicated by the black dot). Follow the direction of the arrows. Finish by overlapping the bias at the under section where you started: **See diagram below.**

Sew down the inside edge first (indicated by a series of dots). The raw edge should flare outward underneath.

start

finish

< **Note:** Cut and apply all applique pieces to this outside edge.

Rotate to complete design.

49

Talt

A lake at the foot of the Ox
mountains in County Sligo.

50

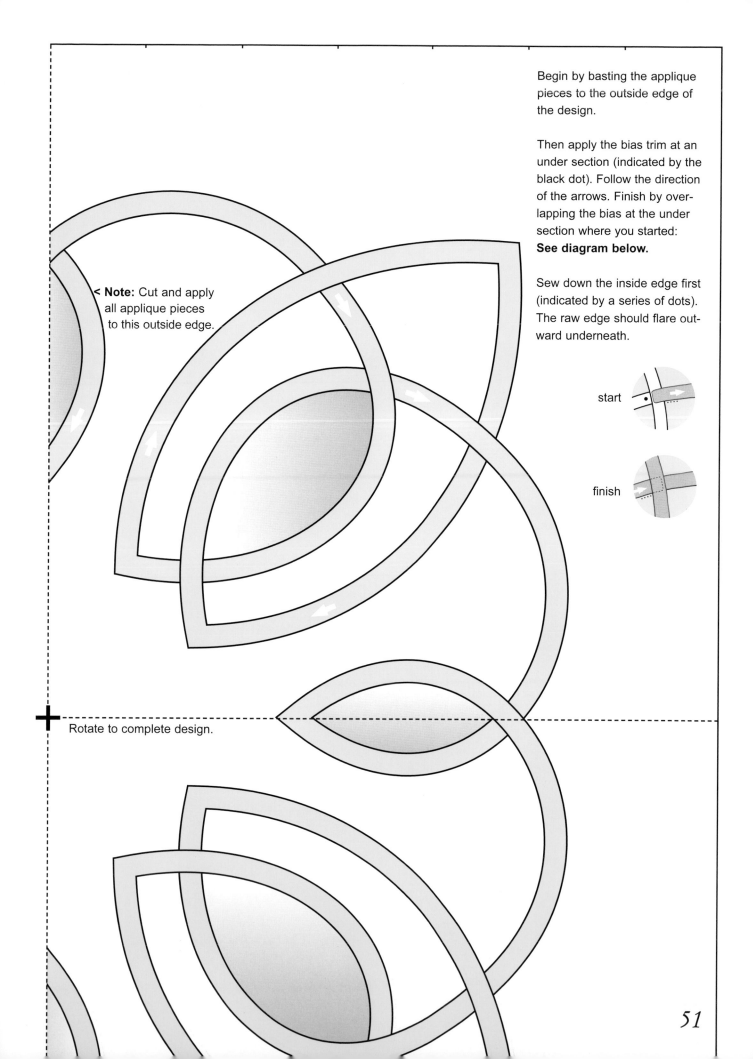

Begin by basting the applique pieces to the outside edge of the design.

Then apply the bias trim at an under section (indicated by the black dot). Follow the direction of the arrows. Finish by overlapping the bias at the under section where you started: **See diagram below.**

Sew down the inside edge first (indicated by a series of dots). The raw edge should flare outward underneath.

start

finish

< **Note:** Cut and apply all applique pieces to this outside edge.

Rotate to complete design.

51

Caher

This tiny island is nestled between
Inis Toirc and the Mayo coast.

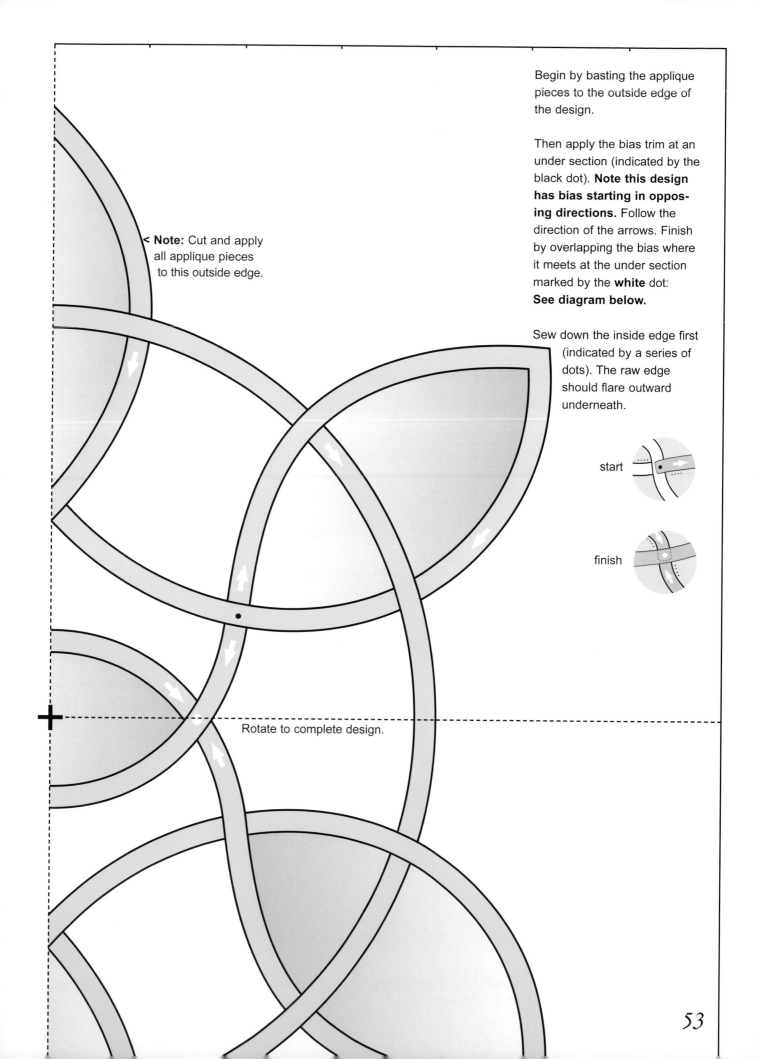

Begin by basting the applique pieces to the outside edge of the design.

Then apply the bias trim at an under section (indicated by the black dot). **Note this design has bias starting in opposing directions.** Follow the direction of the arrows. Finish by overlapping the bias where it meets at the under section marked by the **white** dot: **See diagram below.**

Sew down the inside edge first (indicated by a series of dots). The raw edge should flare outward underneath.

< **Note:** Cut and apply all applique pieces to this outside edge.

start

finish

Rotate to complete design.

53

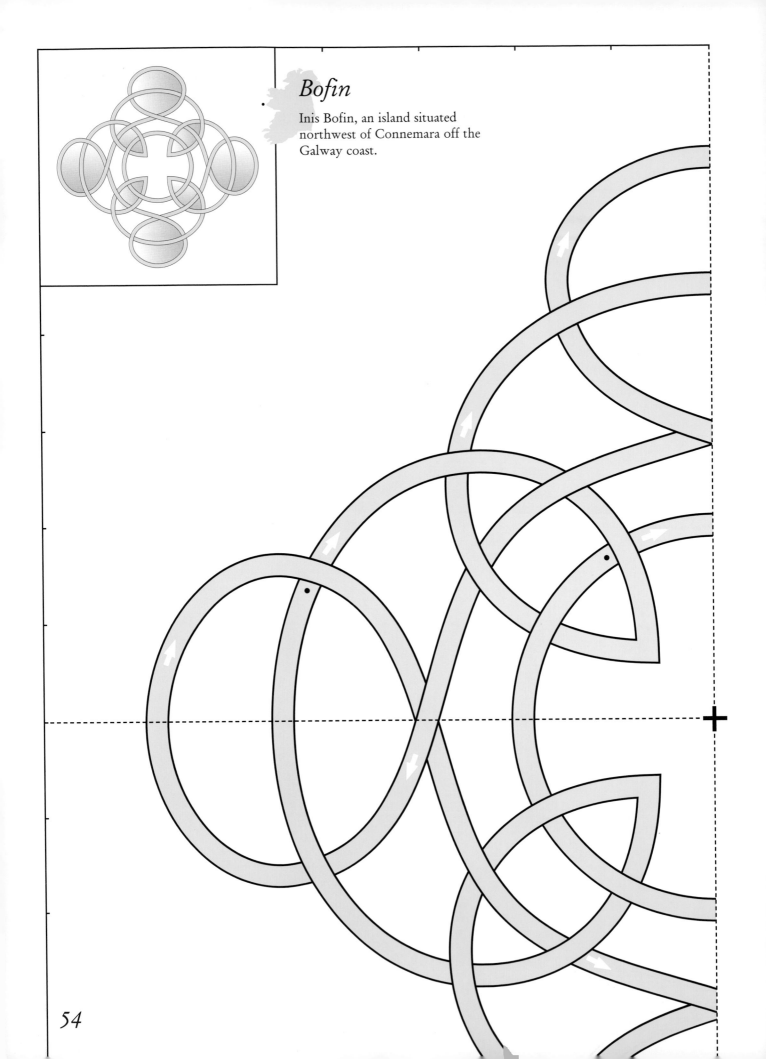

Bofin

Inis Bofin, an island situated
northwest of Connemara off the
Galway coast.

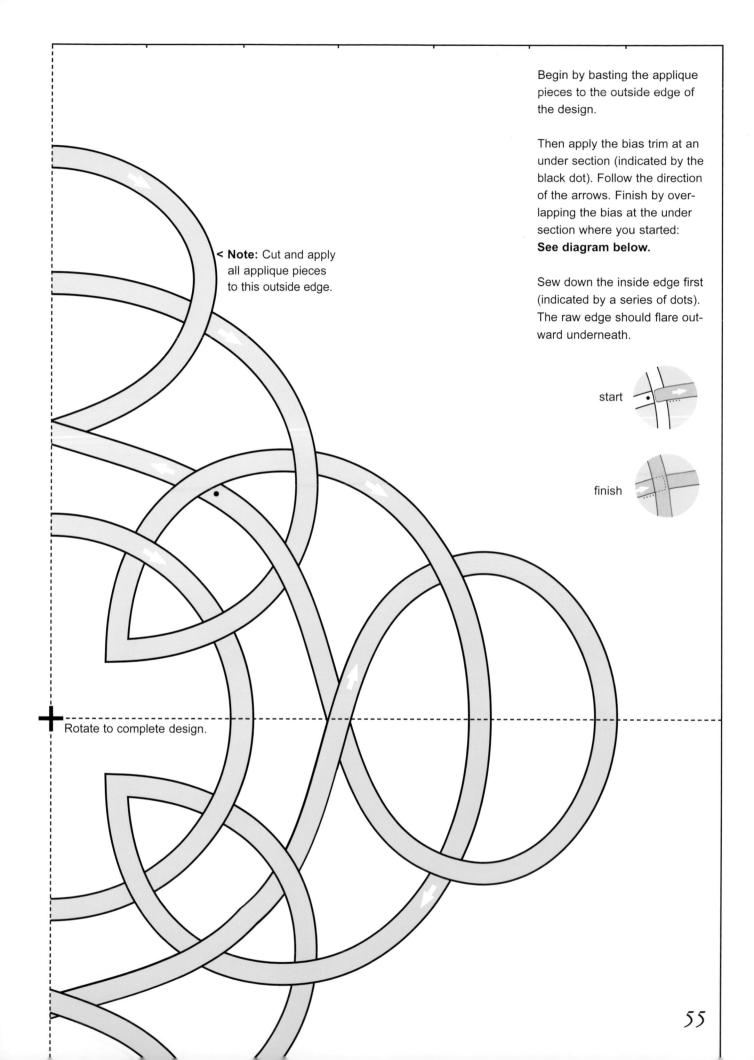

Begin by basting the applique pieces to the outside edge of the design.

Then apply the bias trim at an under section (indicated by the black dot). Follow the direction of the arrows. Finish by overlapping the bias at the under section where you started: **See diagram below.**

Sew down the inside edge first (indicated by a series of dots). The raw edge should flare outward underneath.

< **Note:** Cut and apply all applique pieces to this outside edge.

start

finish

Rotate to complete design.

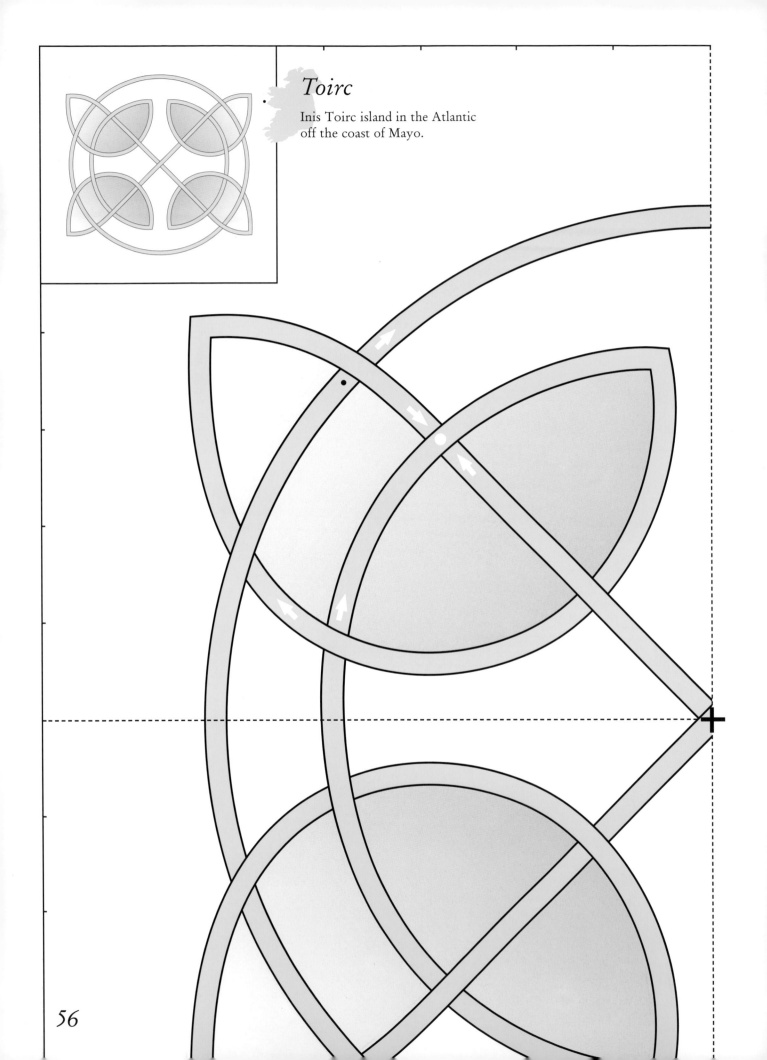

Toirc

Inis Toirc island in the Atlantic
off the coast of Mayo.

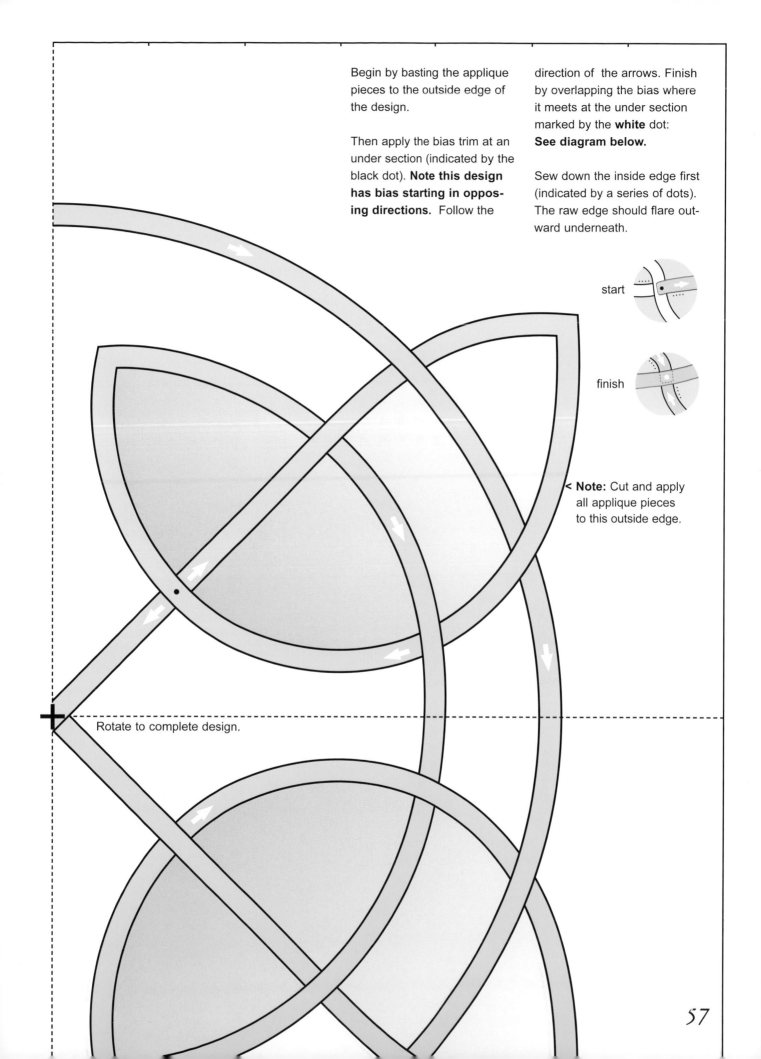

Begin by basting the applique pieces to the outside edge of the design.

Then apply the bias trim at an under section (indicated by the black dot). **Note this design has bias starting in opposing directions.** Follow the direction of the arrows. Finish by overlapping the bias where it meets at the under section marked by the **white** dot: **See diagram below.**

Sew down the inside edge first (indicated by a series of dots). The raw edge should flare outward underneath.

start

finish

< **Note:** Cut and apply all applique pieces to this outside edge.

Rotate to complete design.

Alltain

A lake at the foot of Errigal, in County Donnegal.

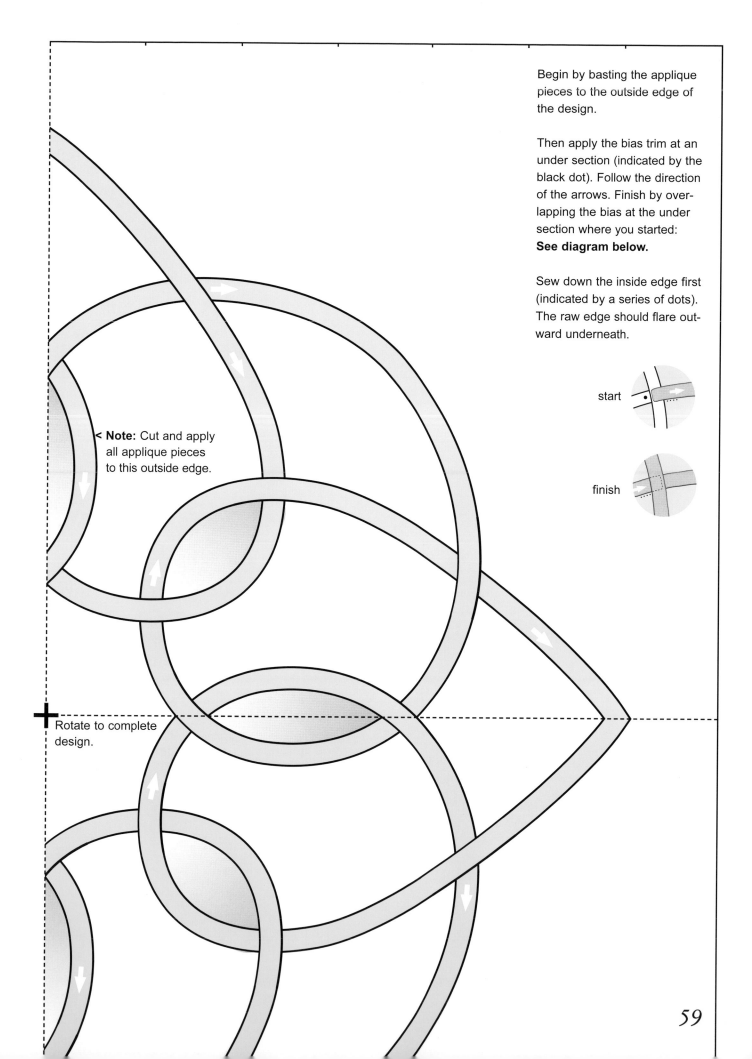

Begin by basting the applique pieces to the outside edge of the design.

Then apply the bias trim at an under section (indicated by the black dot). Follow the direction of the arrows. Finish by over-lapping the bias at the under section where you started: **See diagram below.**

Sew down the inside edge first (indicated by a series of dots). The raw edge should flare out-ward underneath.

start

finish

< **Note:** Cut and apply all applique pieces to this outside edge.

Rotate to complete design.

59

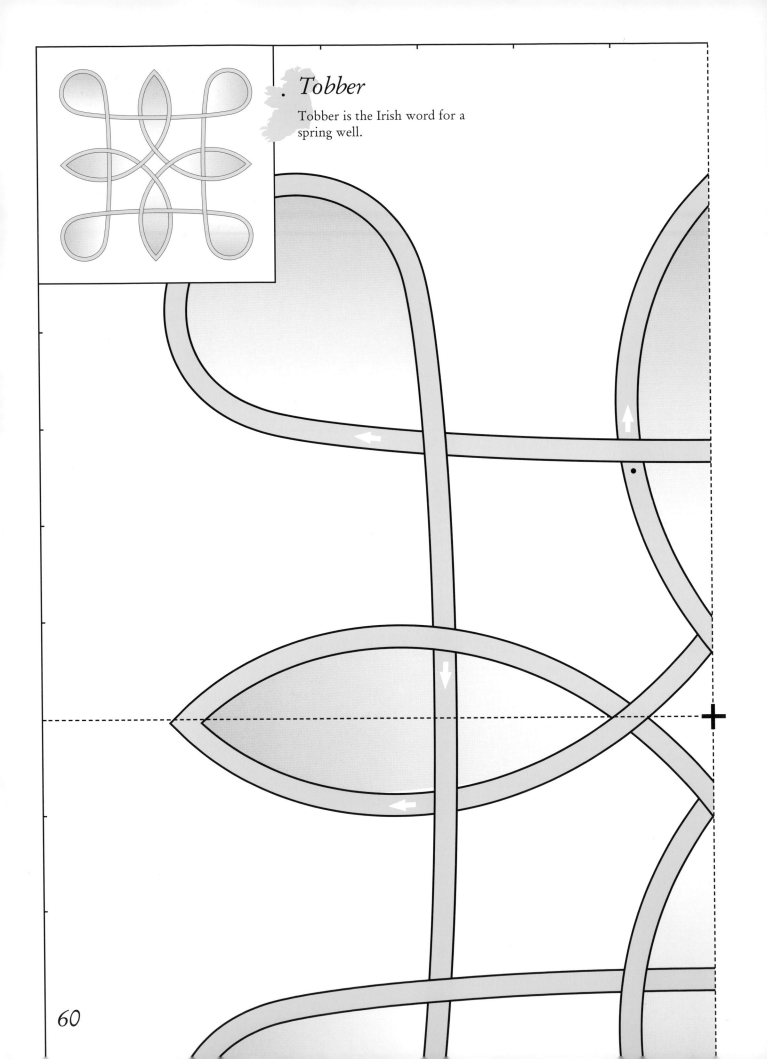

Tobber

Tobber is the Irish word for a spring well.

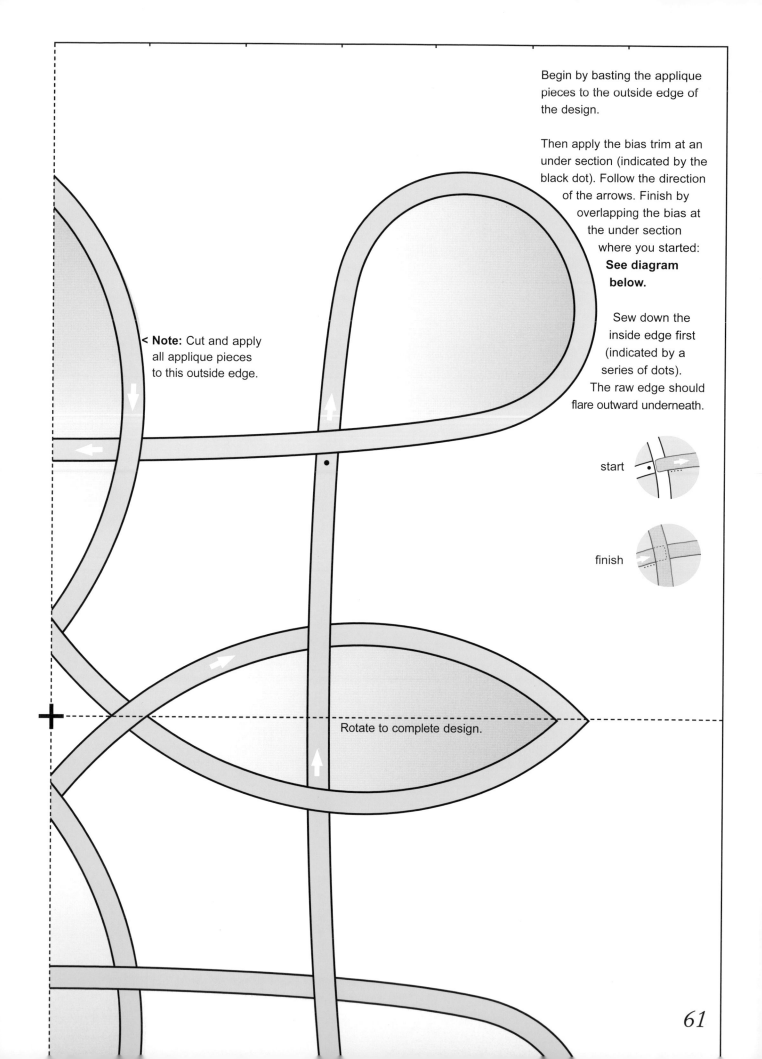

Begin by basting the applique pieces to the outside edge of the design.

Then apply the bias trim at an under section (indicated by the black dot). Follow the direction of the arrows. Finish by overlapping the bias at the under section where you started: **See diagram below.**

Sew down the inside edge first (indicated by a series of dots). The raw edge should flare outward underneath.

< **Note:** Cut and apply all applique pieces to this outside edge.

start

finish

Rotate to complete design.

Aran

Aran, the main island at the
entrance to Galway Bay.

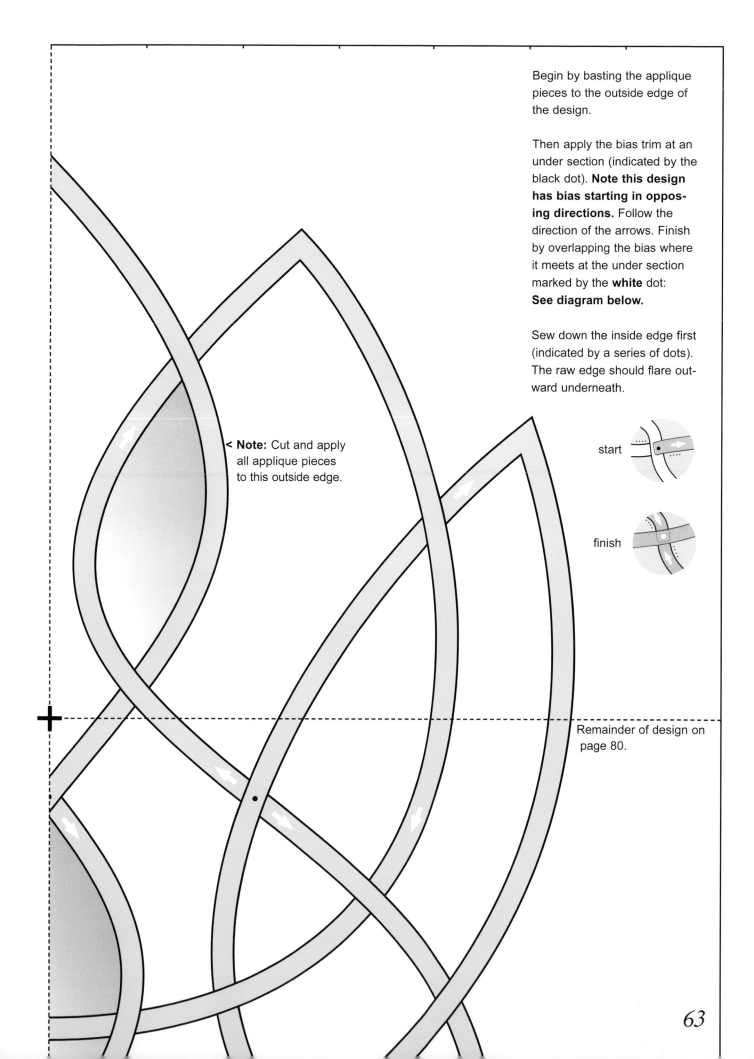

Begin by basting the applique pieces to the outside edge of the design.

Then apply the bias trim at an under section (indicated by the black dot). **Note this design has bias starting in opposing directions.** Follow the direction of the arrows. Finish by overlapping the bias where it meets at the under section marked by the **white** dot: **See diagram below.**

Sew down the inside edge first (indicated by a series of dots). The raw edge should flare outward underneath.

start

finish

< **Note:** Cut and apply all applique pieces to this outside edge.

Remainder of design on page 80.

63

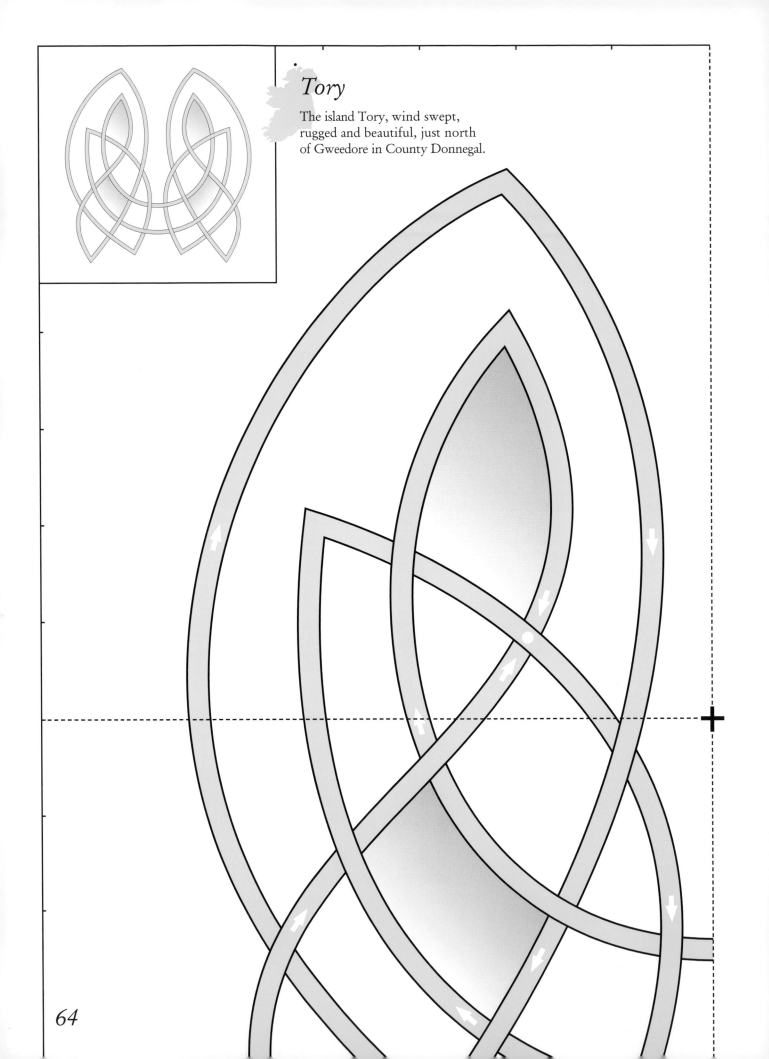

Tory

The island Tory, wind swept, rugged and beautiful, just north of Gweedore in County Donnegal.

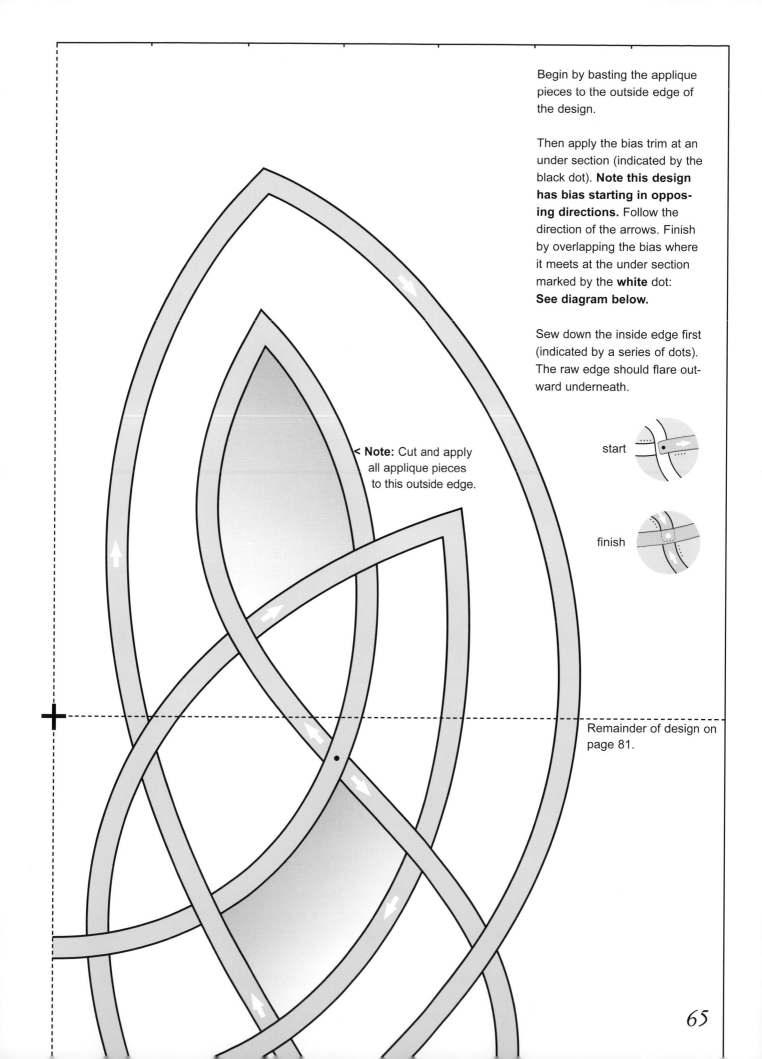

Begin by basting the applique pieces to the outside edge of the design.

Then apply the bias trim at an under section (indicated by the black dot). **Note this design has bias starting in opposing directions.** Follow the direction of the arrows. Finish by overlapping the bias where it meets at the under section marked by the **white** dot: **See diagram below.**

Sew down the inside edge first (indicated by a series of dots). The raw edge should flare outward underneath.

< Note: Cut and apply all applique pieces to this outside edge.

start

finish

Remainder of design on page 81.

65

Owey

Owey, the lonely island, south-west of Gweedore.

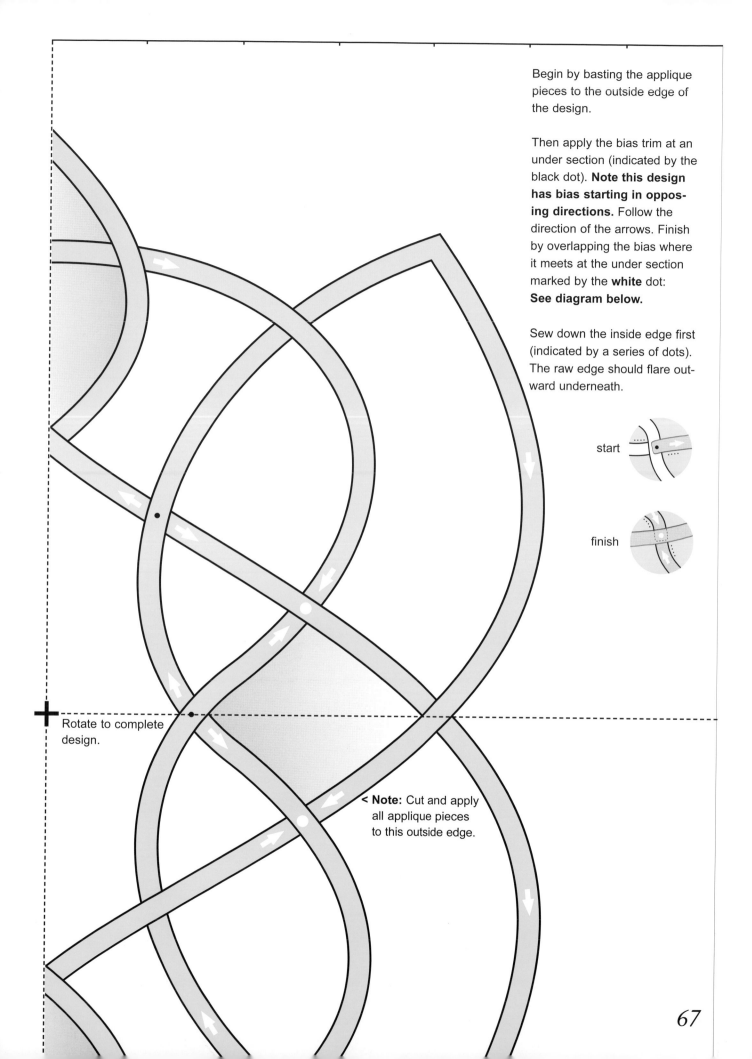

Begin by basting the applique pieces to the outside edge of the design.

Then apply the bias trim at an under section (indicated by the black dot). **Note this design has bias starting in opposing directions.** Follow the direction of the arrows. Finish by overlapping the bias where it meets at the under section marked by the **white** dot: **See diagram below.**

Sew down the inside edge first (indicated by a series of dots). The raw edge should flare outward underneath.

start

finish

Rotate to complete design.

< **Note:** Cut and apply all applique pieces to this outside edge.

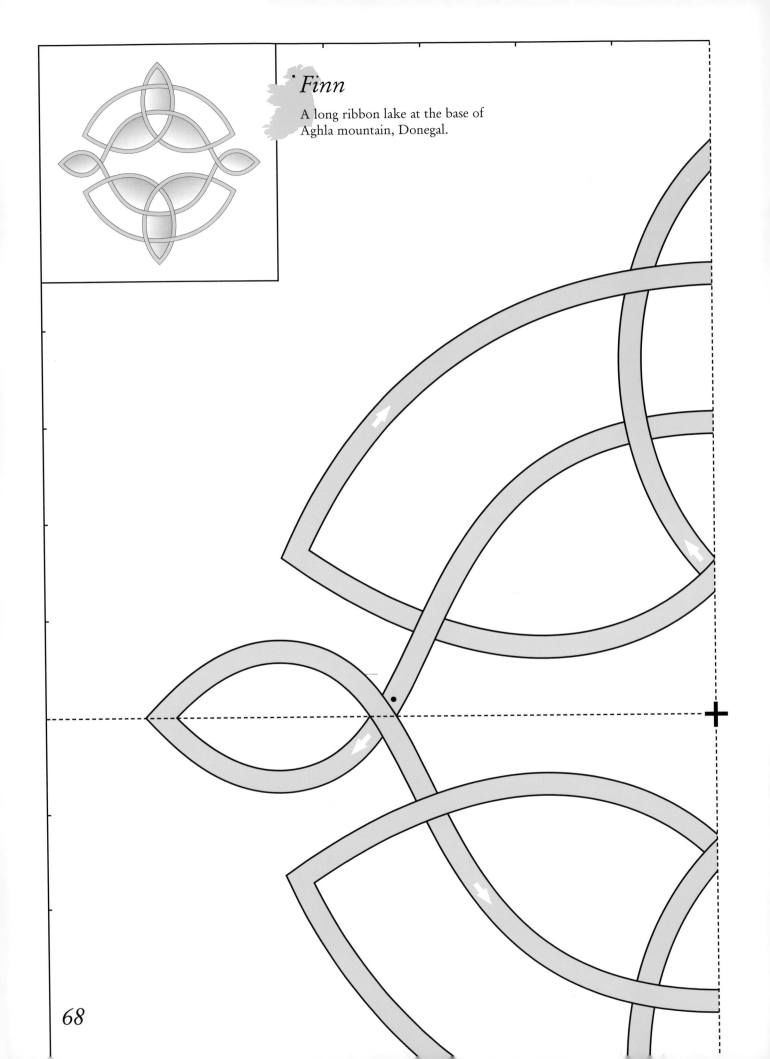

Finn

A long ribbon lake at the base of
Aghla mountain, Donegal.

68

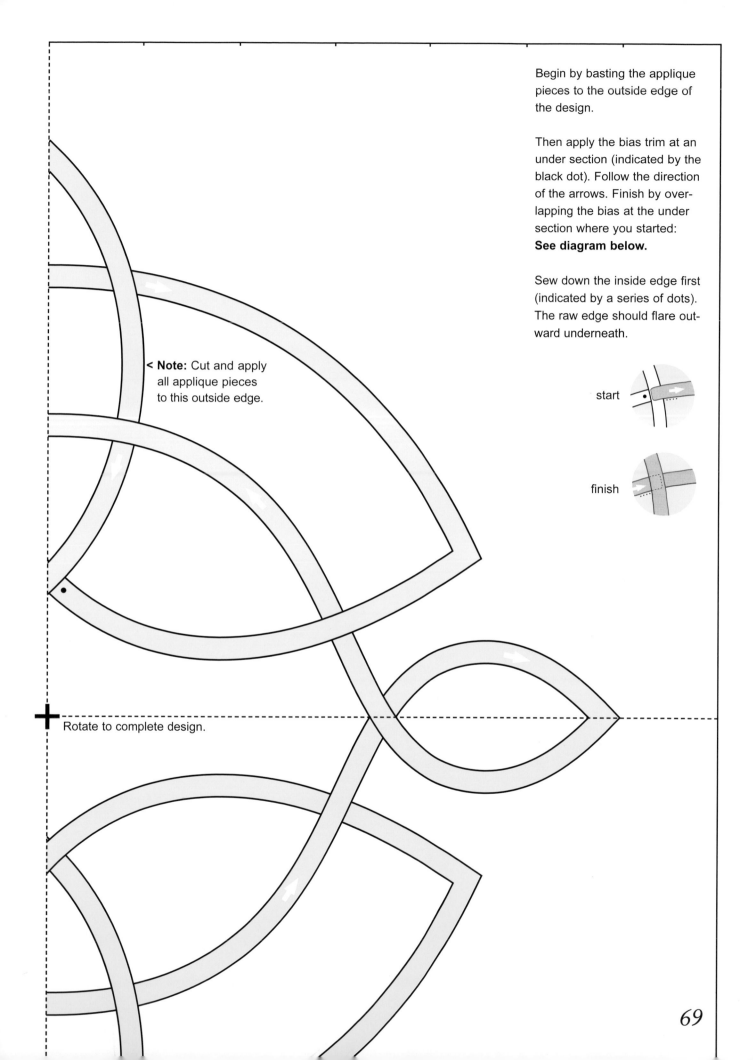

Begin by basting the applique pieces to the outside edge of the design.

Then apply the bias trim at an under section (indicated by the black dot). Follow the direction of the arrows. Finish by over-lapping the bias at the under section where you started: **See diagram below.**

Sew down the inside edge first (indicated by a series of dots). The raw edge should flare out-ward underneath.

start

finish

< **Note:** Cut and apply all applique pieces to this outside edge.

Rotate to complete design.

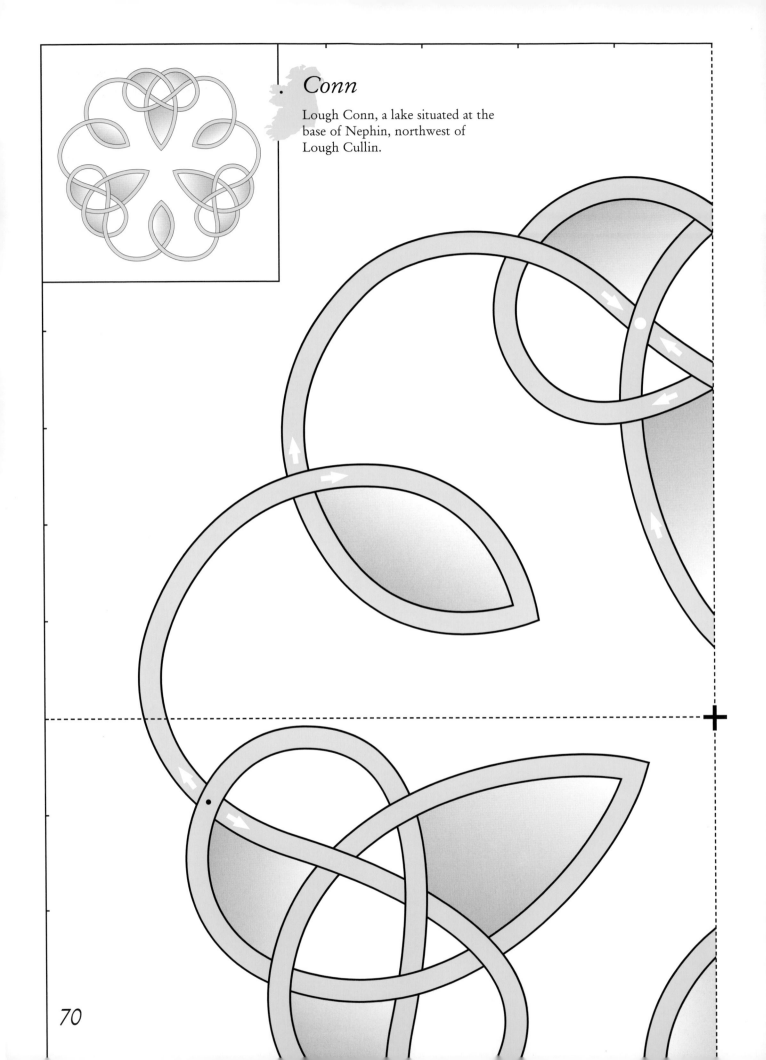

Conn

Lough Conn, a lake situated at the base of Nephin, northwest of Lough Cullin.

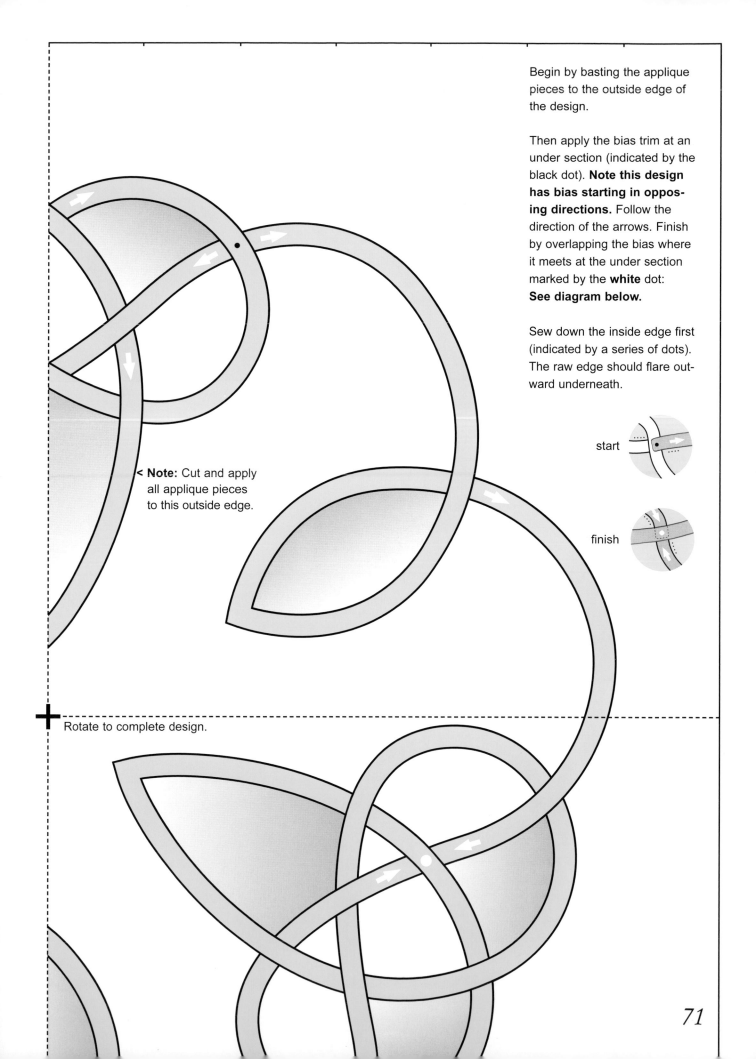

Begin by basting the applique pieces to the outside edge of the design.

Then apply the bias trim at an under section (indicated by the black dot). **Note this design has bias starting in opposing directions.** Follow the direction of the arrows. Finish by overlapping the bias where it meets at the under section marked by the **white** dot: **See diagram below.**

Sew down the inside edge first (indicated by a series of dots). The raw edge should flare outward underneath.

start

finish

< **Note:** Cut and apply all applique pieces to this outside edge.

Rotate to complete design.

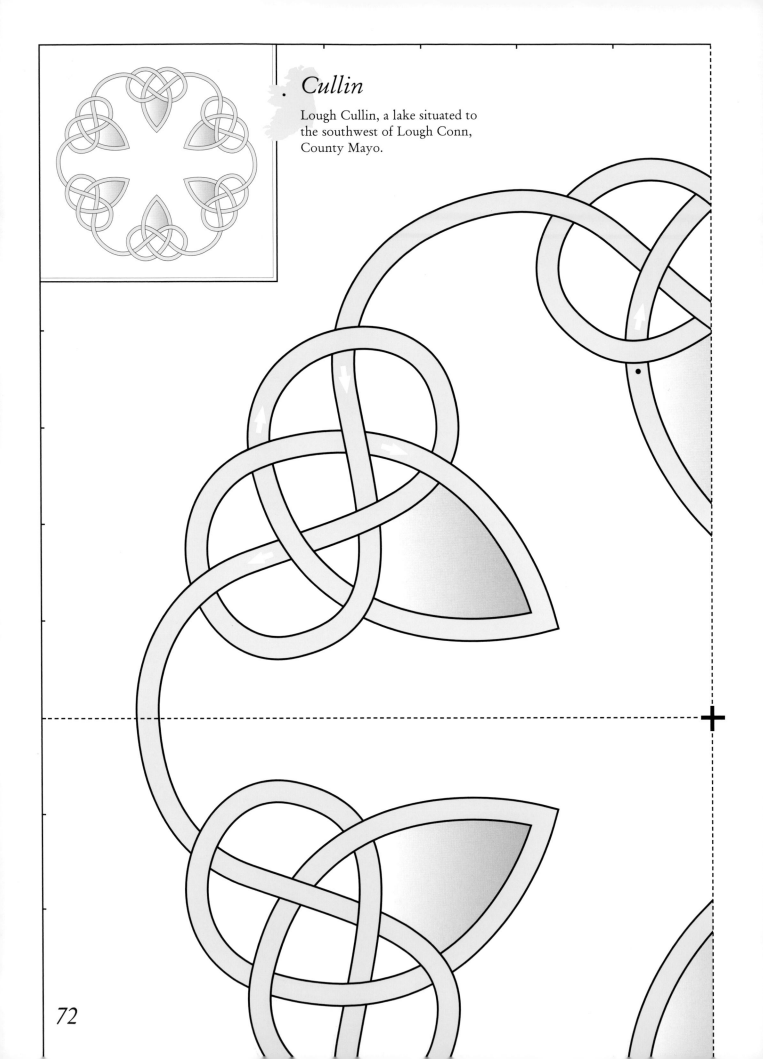

Cullin

Lough Cullin, a lake situated to
the southwest of Lough Conn,
County Mayo.

72

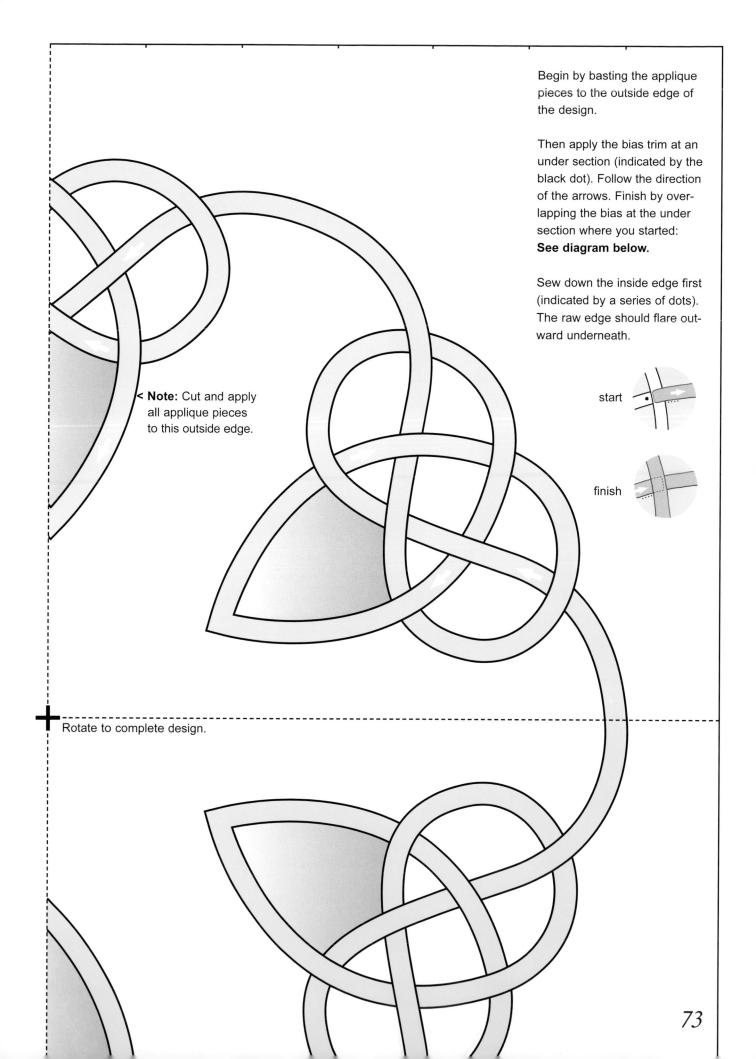

Begin by basting the applique pieces to the outside edge of the design.

Then apply the bias trim at an under section (indicated by the black dot). Follow the direction of the arrows. Finish by over-lapping the bias at the under section where you started: **See diagram below.**

Sew down the inside edge first (indicated by a series of dots). The raw edge should flare out-ward underneath.

start

finish

< **Note:** Cut and apply all applique pieces to this outside edge.

Rotate to complete design.

Carra

Lough Carra, a lake dotted with dozens of islands, just north of Lough Mask.

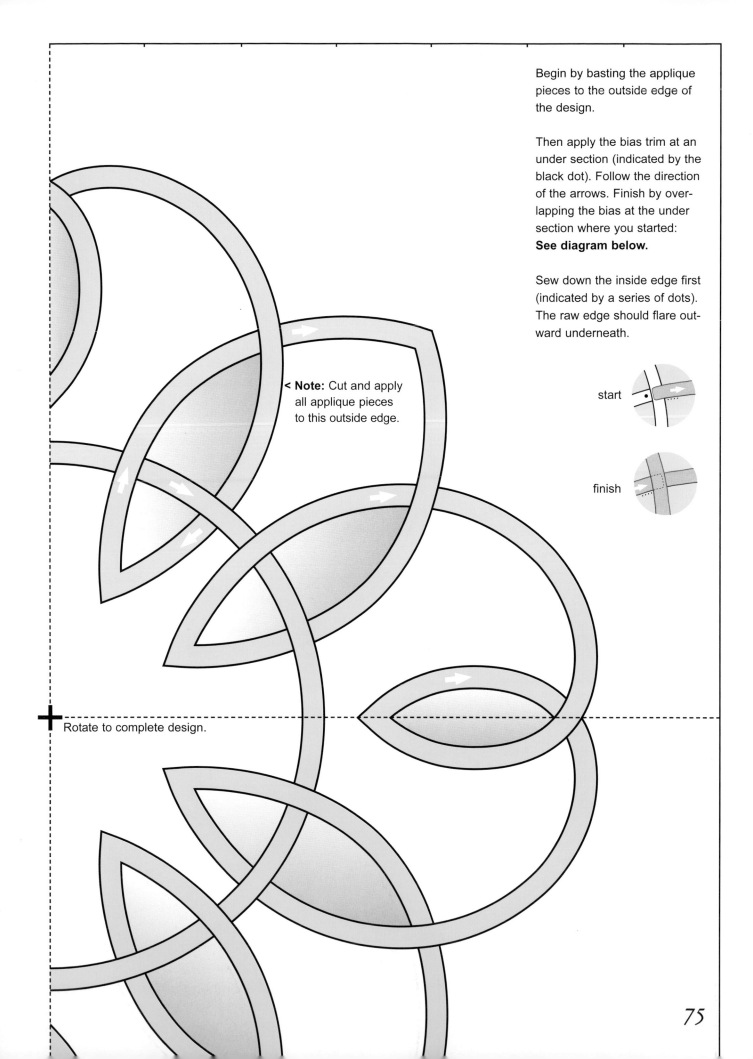

Begin by basting the applique pieces to the outside edge of the design.

Then apply the bias trim at an under section (indicated by the black dot). Follow the direction of the arrows. Finish by overlapping the bias at the under section where you started: **See diagram below.**

Sew down the inside edge first (indicated by a series of dots). The raw edge should flare outward underneath.

start

finish

< **Note:** Cut and apply all applique pieces to this outside edge.

Rotate to complete design.

75

Achill

An island situated in the west
pointing out into the Atlantic.

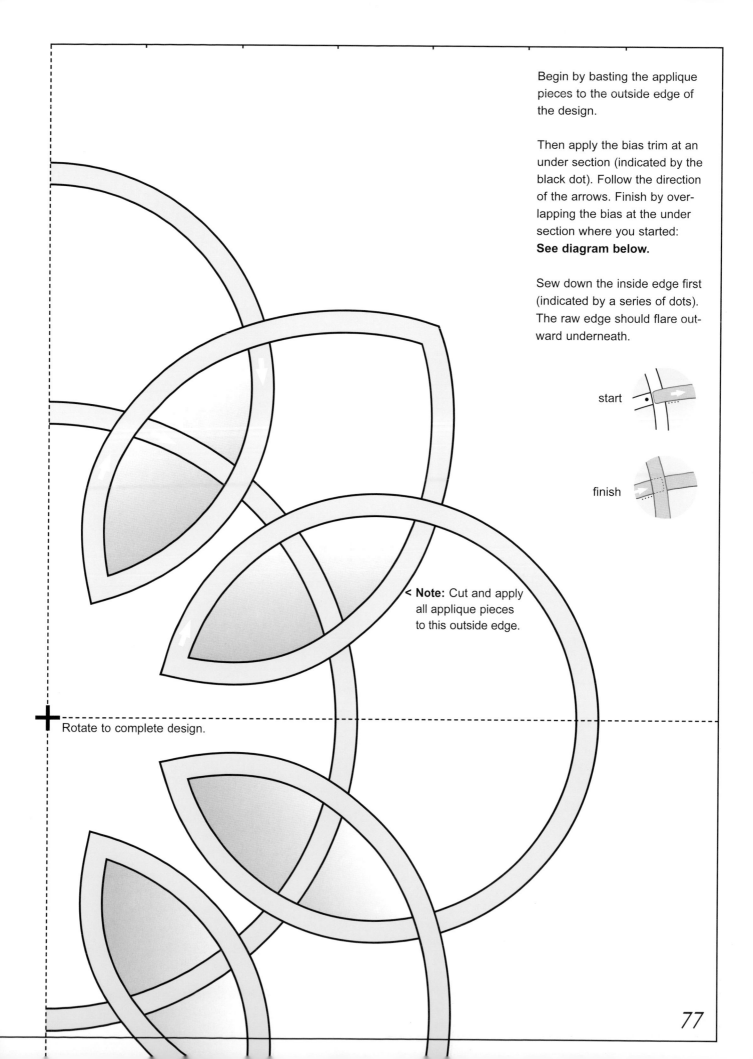

Begin by basting the applique pieces to the outside edge of the design.

Then apply the bias trim at an under section (indicated by the black dot). Follow the direction of the arrows. Finish by overlapping the bias at the under section where you started: **See diagram below.**

Sew down the inside edge first (indicated by a series of dots). The raw edge should flare outward underneath.

start

finish

< **Note:** Cut and apply all applique pieces to this outside edge.

Rotate to complete design.

King Lir This way up

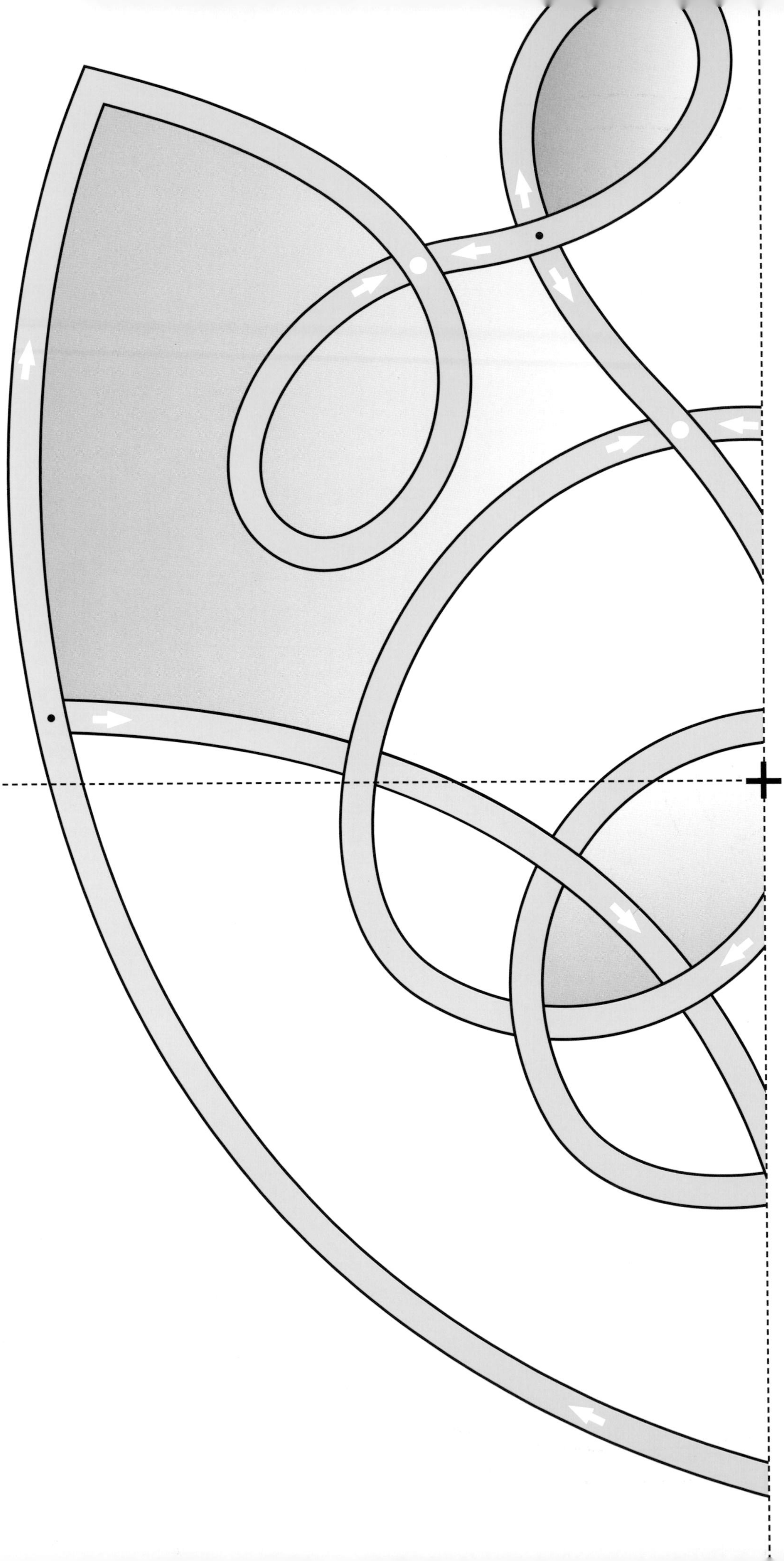

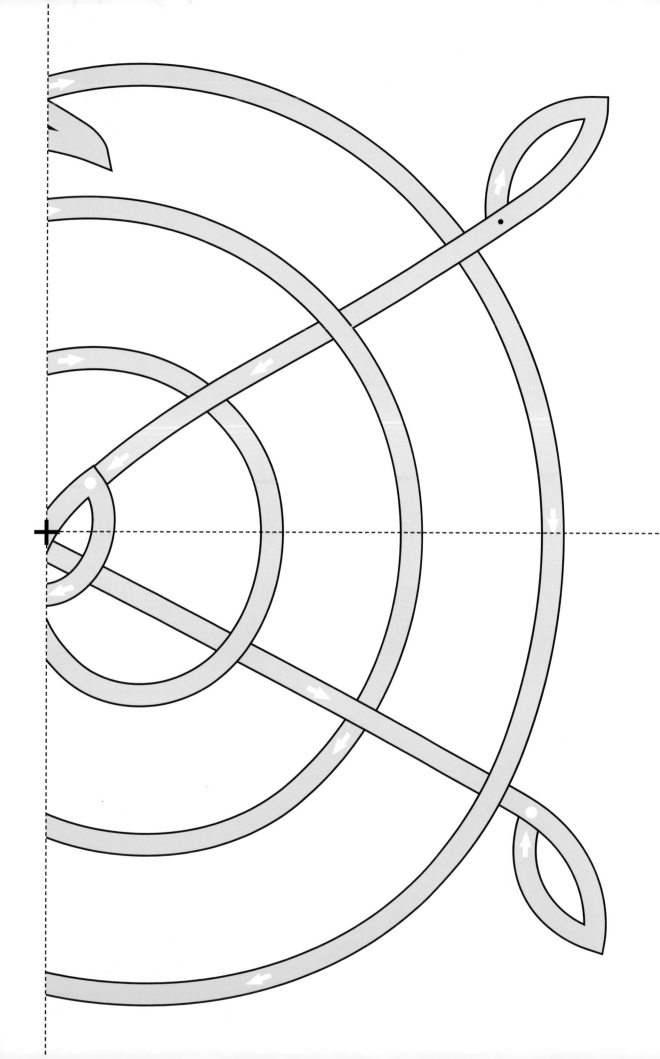

79

Aran This way up

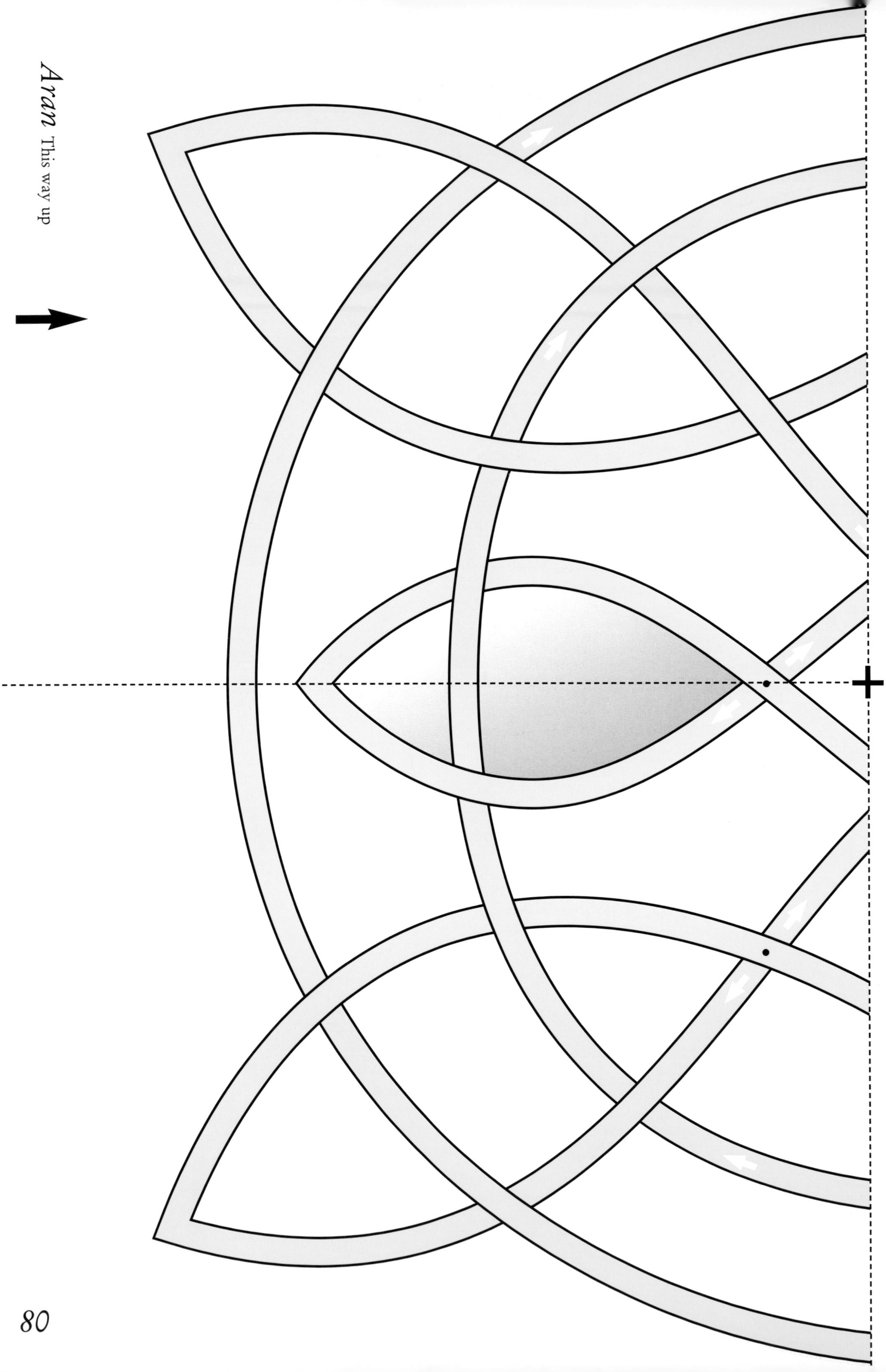

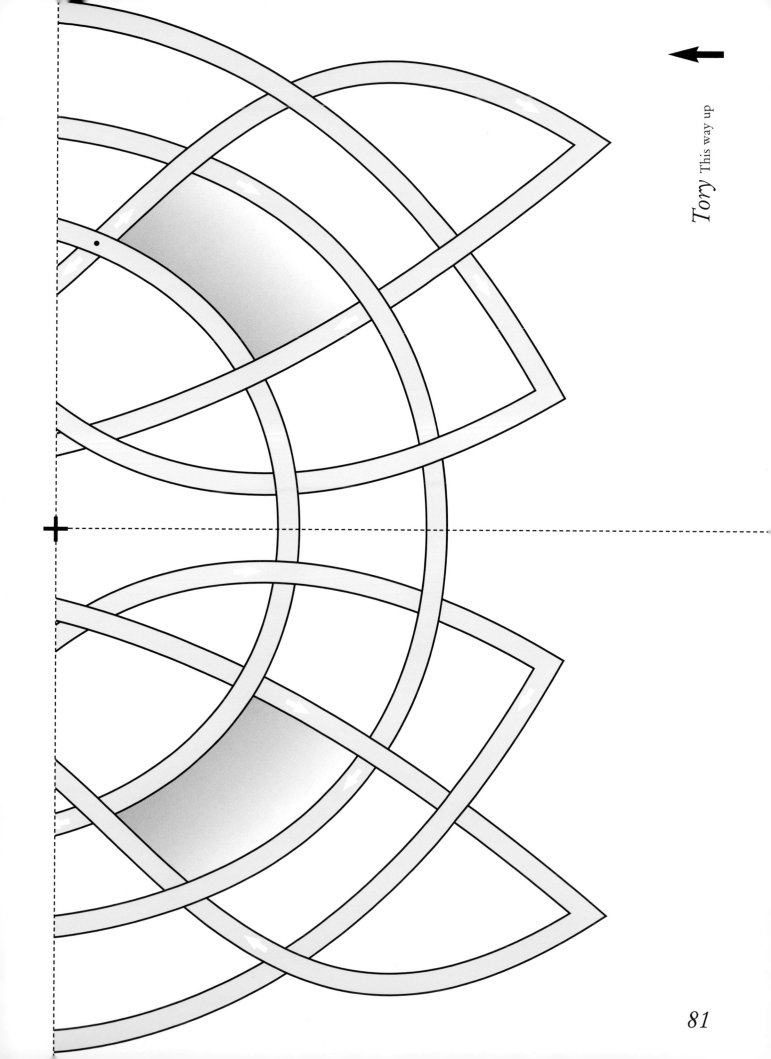

Acknowledgments

Teaching and lecturing about Celtic design and quilting has enabled me to visit so many interesting and lovely places and meet with quilters throughout the United States, Canada, Europe, Australia, Ireland and the British Isles. My sincerest appreciation to all my students and followers who bought the earlier books on interlace, spirals and floral. It is you who inspired me to develop *Celtic Quilt Design II* and it is to you that this book is dedicated.

I thank Louise Horkey of Whiffle Tree Quilts for allowing me to use her classroom and the Santa Clara County fair quilters (Wednesday group) who met at her shop on a weekly basis to help me work out the kinks in my Celtic Rose Window. Several of the ladies participated, Fay Meyers, Nancy Young, Nancy Kon, Louise Horkey, Barbara Amedo and Shirley Estrada, and all did wonderful work. Shirley made Variation #1 of Celtic Rose Window, which won a blue ribbon at the California State Fair in Sacramento and is currently on exhibit at the governor's office in the capitol building in Sacramento.

A big thank you to students Joan Blomquist, Pat Daughters and Sherry Klootwyk for allowing me to include photographs of their work in the book.

Thanks, Joan, for keeping me on track on a day-to-day basis.

A special thank you to my friend Pat Flynn Kyser for the time she spent with me editing the book and Crystal Chow who did the copy editing. A big thank you to my nephew, Colm Sweetman, for his talented design skills. They have all stood by and supported me throughout the project.

My grateful thanks to Hau Thi Long and my niece Grainne Keating for their help and support over the years.

A special thank you to my dear friend Marmie Schraub for her support and love over the years. Life is always a better place with her around.

I would also like to applaud the many unique quilt shops throughout the world that carry my books, stencils and bias bars. They do a wonderful job retailing the fabrics and tools of the trade, and of furthering the art of quilting. I hope you visit them often. They are exciting places to shop.

Bibliography

Barnes, Christine. *Color the Quilters Guide,* That Patchwork Place, Inc. Bothell, WA. 1997.

Beyer, Jenny. *Color Confidence for Quilters.* The Quilt Digest Press, NTC/Contemporary Publishing Company, Chicago, IL.

Birren, Faber. *Creative Color, A Dynamic Approach for Artists and Designers,* Schiffer Publishing Ltd., West Chester, PA, 1987.

Itten, Johannes. *The Elements of Color,* Van Nostrand Reinhold, NY, 1970.

Mitchell G. Frank and Harbison, Peter. *Treasures of Irish Art, 1500 B.C to1500 A .D.,* The Metropolitan Museum of Art & Alfred A. Knopf, NY, 1997.

Martin, Judy and McCloskey, Marsha. Pieced Borders, The Complete Resource, Corsley-Griffith Publishing Co., Inc., Grunnell, IA. (c 1994)

Zaczek, Iain. *Irish Legends*, Contemporary Books NTC/Contemporary Publishing Group Inc. Chicago, IL, 1998.

Quilting Periodicals

American Quilter, American Quilters Society, P.O. Box 3290 Paducha, KY 42002-9949.

Better Homes and Gardens, American Patchwork & Quilting by Meredith Corporation, 1716 Locust St., Des Moines, IA 50309-3023.

Quilters Newsletter Magazine, Primedia, Inc. 741 Corporate Circle Suite A, Golden, CO 80401.

Sources

Start at your local quilt shop. If after checking there you find you are still searching for that special piece of fabric or a particular tool, this brief list of sources may help:

Alaska Dyeworks, P.O. Box 697, 322 Ogden St., Village of Oxford, NE 68967-0697. A wide variety of hand-dyed fabrics.

Artspoken Yardage, Marit Lee Kucera, St., Paul, MN 651-222-2483. A wonderful selection of hand-dyed 100% cotton fabrics.

Celtic Design Company, P. O Box 2643, Sunnyvale, CA 94087. Metal Bias Bars (1/8", 3/16", 1/4", 3/8", 1/2", 5/8" and 3/4"), books, patterns and stencils.

Checker Distributors, 400-B West Dussel Drive, Maumee, OH 43537. Serving quilt shops around the world with all quilter needs, including Celtic products.

FABRICSTODYEFOR.COM Hand-painted 100% pima cotton.

Quilters Resource, Inc., 2211 N Elston Avenue, Chicago, IL 60614 Serving quilt shops around the world with all quilter needs, including Celtic products.

StenSource International, 18971 Hess Ave., Sonora, CA 95370. Serving quilt shops throughout the world with over 2,000 stencils to choose from, including Celtic stencils. www.stensource.com